TIGER ROLL

THE LITTLE LEGEND

RACING POST
— LEGENDS —

TIGER ROLL

THE LITTLE LEGEND

EDITED BY ANDREW PENNINGTON

With thanks to Randox Health for its valued support

First published in Great Britain in 2019 by
Racing Post Books
27 Kingfisher Court, Hambridge Road, Newbury, Berkshire, RG14 5SJ

10 9 8 7 6 5 4 3 2 1

A catalogue record for this book is available from the British Library.

ISBN 978-1-83950-032-9

Designed by John Schwartz
Cover designed by Jay Vincent

Printed and bound in Slovenia by DZS Grafik, Ljubljana

www.racingpost.com/shop

Photographic acknowledgements
All the photos are copyright Racing Post except the following:
Alain Barr: pages 34, 35 and 45
Caroline Norris: pages 14, 87 and 107 (top)
Getty Images: pages 6, 12-13, 20-21, 42-43, 60-61, 68, 104, 120-121 and 126-127
Grossick Racing: pages 51, 52-53, 54, 56-57, 62, 64, 71, 72-73, 76, 77, 90, 95, 97, 116-117,
    143, 156, 158, 159, 160 and 162
Jerry O'Brien: page 9
Mark Cranham and Gerry Cranham: pages 40 and 140
Martin Lynch: page 25
Back jacket: Edward Whitaker (top left), Getty Images (top right), Grossick Racing
    (bottom left and bottom right)

CONTENTS

FOREWORD

by DR PETER FITZGERALD

I t is an honour to introduce this edition of Racing Post 'Legends', to mark the true legend that is two-time Randox Health Grand National winner Tiger Roll.

His fairytale story of determination and dedication will be forever etched in the history books of Aintree racecourse and steeplechase racing, and I am so pleased that the team and I at Randox Health were able to be a part of it, and to witness history in the making.

On that celebrated day – Saturday, April 6, 2019 – the atmosphere was electric and the cheers of the crowd deafening as Tiger Roll, steered by his jockey Davy Russell, stretched himself ahead of the competition to become the first consecutive winner of this most famous race since the days of Red Rum.

I would therefore like to take this opportunity to say another hearty congratulations to the small but mighty Tiger Roll, Davy, trainer Gordon Elliott, and owner Michael O'Leary, whose tireless work and passion saw their much-loved horse storm to victory for a second time.

Tiger Roll's dual win at the Randox Health Grand National confirmed what we have all known for quite some time – that it is stories such as this one that transcend the sport of racing, make it so special, and give it its wide-reaching appeal.

Tiger Roll, racing's newest star, is rightfully loved by jockeys, grooms, trainers, and owners for his ability to defy the odds and deliver when it matters most, but he has just as important a place in the hearts of racing fans, families and even children, for his absolute fearlessness, his strength of character and his love of the cameras.

Opposite page: Tiger Roll and Davy Russell clear the final fence in the Grand National at Aintree in April 2018

What Gordon Elliott said of him is completely true. He is 'The People's Horse' and his back-to-back wins have forever secured the Randox Health Grand National's place as 'The People's Race.'

For that reason we have for three years now been delighted to partner with the Jockey Club and Aintree to bring this race to the millions who avidly await the unfolding of the event.

Our partnership with the Randox Health Grand National is an opportunity for us to spread our message of preventative health, but it is also a chance to show our commitment, at a national level, to this wonderful sport. I have been a keen equestrian all my life and Randox, historically, has given its name to many local point-to-point and polo meetings near our headquarters in Northern Ireland.

It's the perfect fit, therefore, to unite our company ethos, of helping people to extend and enjoy their lives, with the People's Race. Together, we can encourage people to live healthier for longer, in order to enjoy events such as the Randox Health Grand National for as long as possible.

I would like to thank the millions who joined us in 2019 – whether in person at Aintree or tuned in to the screen or airwaves – and hope that you enjoy this book, which serves to recognise that memorable day for years to come.

We look forward to continuing our partnership in the coming years as we deliver the world's most famous steeplechase, share our preventative health message, and of course cheer on the talented horses and riders who take to the course to reach for the glory of being crowned winner of the Randox Health Grand National.

Each year holds the promise of creating another legend like Tiger Roll and I cannot wait to see into whose hands I will present the coveted Randox Health Grand National trophy in 2020.

Dr Peter FitzGerald, Randox Health Founder and Managing Director, September 2019

INTRODUCTION

by ANDREW PENNINGTON

Tiger Roll has achieved a standing that few racehorses attain – he has become a household name, a people's horse. It is a place reserved for racehorses who accomplish extraordinary things. The names who occupy this unique position in the hearts of the public form a roll call of the most famous names to have graced the jumping game in the last 60 years – Arkle, Red Rum and Desert Orchid.

It is, of course, fitting that Red Rum is among that trio for he is the Aintree legend whom Tiger Roll emulated on that glorious afternoon in April 2019. Forty-five years after Ginger McCain's titan of the sport landed what turned out to be the second of three Grand Nationals, Tiger Roll won back-to-back runnings of the world's most famous steeplechase.

It's not just the fact he won a second National, it was the manner of his victory for such a small horse that stood out, with the unique challenge of the iconic spruce fences sparking something special inside.

To reach that peak Tiger Roll has taken his connections on a scarcely believable journey and, while most of the names in this wonderful story are familiar, one is possibly not – Sheikh Mohammed.

Tiger Roll – like Red Rum – was bred to race on the Flat but he failed to see the racecourse in nearly three years with the sheikh's Godolphin operation. It was West Country trainer Nigel Hawke, himself a Grand National winner on Seagram in 1991, who then guided Tiger Roll to his maiden success at Market Rasen in November 2013.

Tiger Roll as a foal

The National theme continued when he was bought by Michael O'Leary's Gigginstown House Stud and was put into training with Gordon Elliott. The County Meath trainer famously won the Aintree showpiece in his first season as a licence holder with Silver Birch in 2007.

Tiger Roll has not just won two Grand Nationals, though, as he has also triumphed at four Cheltenham Festivals over different trips and in different disciplines. He has entered the hallowed winner's enclosure at Prestbury Park following victories in the Triumph Hurdle, the National Hunt Chase and twice after the Cross Country Chase.

Elliott has guided him to an unparalleled career and helped provide unforgettable moments in the careers of jockeys Lisa O'Neill and Keith Donoghue.

However, it is Davy Russell who will be remembered most as the rider who partnered Tiger Roll to those famous Grand National wins and ensured his name stands alongside the legends of the past. Those two victories will stand long in the memory.

This is a remarkable story about a remarkable horse.

Opposite page: Tiger Roll at Gordon Elliott's County Meath stables

1
Winning start

C *heers at Cheltenham and adulation at Aintree were far from*
Jerry O'Brien's thoughts in 2009 when he arranged the mating
of his mare Swiss Roll with Authorized, who two years earlier
famously provided Frankie Dettori with his first victory in the Derby. Alan
Sweetman takes up the story:

Jerry O'Brien worked for nearly three decades as a veterinary
surgeon at Coolmore Stud. His expertise was in the field of
reproduction and it was natural he began to dabble in breeding.
One of the mares he bought was On Air, who had won a couple
of mile-and-a-quarter races and a novice hurdle in 1994 for Nick
Gaselee.

On Air produced four winners, all trained by Tommy Stack.
If that now looks like something of an omen for what Tiger Roll
went on to achieve, it is worth mentioning that one of them, named
Khachaturian, later won four races for Donald McCain. Stack,
McCain – names indelibly linked with Red Rum, the greatest Grand
National story of all.

Yes, maybe the fates were already conspiring.

The best of On Air's foals was Berenson, a colt by Entrepreneur.
He won a maiden first time out at the Curragh in August 2004.
The following month he finished second to Dubawi in the Group 1
National Stakes and Godolphin bought him. He never ran again.

At that stage Berenson's sister Swiss Roll was still racing. She
won a maiden at three and a conditions race at four at the 2004
Galway festival.

Continuing in training at five, she achieved black type when
second in the Listed Vintage Crop Stakes at Navan in May 2005.

In 2009 Swiss Roll produced a colt foal by Dubawi called
Ahzeemah who was bought for 60,000gns by John Ferguson. He
went into training with Godolphin and ended up winning five

Jerry O'Brien, the breeder of Tiger Roll

Tiger Roll's half-brother Ahzeemah (near side) wins the Lonsdale Cup at York in August 2013

races, including a narrow defeat of the Willie Mullins-trained Simenon in the Group 2 Lonsdale Cup at York in August 2013.

Her next mating was with Authorized, and the resultant foal was bought by Ferguson for 70,000gns at the Tattersalls foal sale in November 2010. He was registered in Sheikh Mohammed's ownership but was unraced when consigned by Darley, now named Tiger Roll, at Doncaster in August 2013.

Nigel Hawke bought Tiger Roll for £10,000 and introduced him in a juvenile hurdle at Market Rasen that November. Starting at 12-1 in a field of five, he took advantage of a poor display by 2-11 favourite Zamoyski to win in promising fashion despite looking a bit green.

RACING POST ANALYSIS – Dave Orton

There was a right turn-up in this seemingly uncompetitive juvenile contest as long odds-on Zamoyski flopped and newcomer Tiger Roll got his career off to a perfect start.

The winner is not from a yard associated with debut scorers, but he was the unknown quantity in the race and took to his task really well. He's got a decent Flat pedigree as well as being a Darley cast-off and he obviously has the requisite stamina. There really should be some more to come as his rider later said he was idling late in the day.

MARKET RASEN
November 10, 2013
1stsecuritysolutions Juvenile Hurdle
2m½f

1	Tiger Roll	Mark Quinlan	12-1
2	Nonotnow	Harry Haynes	7-1
3	Zamoyski	Richard Johnson	2-11f

3¾ lengths, 8 lengths
5 ran

One month after that debut success Tiger Roll was back at the sales. This time it was Brightwells at Cheltenham, where Mags O'Toole, the bloodstock agent and daughter of legendary Irish trainer Mick O'Toole, bought him for £80,000 on behalf of Gigginstown House Stud, bound for the yard of Gordon Elliott.

As Elliott got to know his new recruit, plans were formulated for the remainder of the season and in early February 2014 Tiger Roll was supplemented for the Grade 1 Gala Retail Spring Juvenile Hurdle at Leopardstown.

It was a huge step up from winning a juvenile hurdle, as Elliott explained before the race: 'We thought it was worth taking the chance in a Grade 1 as there are so few opportunities for four-year-olds to run in anything else once they have lost their maiden tags.'

Tiger Roll was sent off a relatively unconsidered 16-1 shot at Leopardstown and finished second to the more experienced Guitar Pete, who had already won a Grade 2 juvenile hurdle.

That peformance gave Elliott plenty of encouragement and he said after the race: 'If Tiger Roll had jumped the last, he wouldn't have beaten the winner but he would have been right on top of him. He'll go for the Triumph and will take in a Grade 2 at Fairyhouse later this month before that.'

As it turned out, he went straight to the Triumph and Bryan Cooper, who rode Tiger Roll in the Spring Juvenile Hurdle and was Gigginstown's number-one jockey, said in the run-up to the Cheltenham Festival that his mount would have solid claims in the opening race on the final day of the meeting.

Cooper said: 'I'm convinced there is plenty of improvement to come from Tiger Roll. Don't forget he was having only his second run when chasing home Guitar Pete in the Spring Juvenile Hurdle and it was his debut for Gordon too. He's been in good form since then and I certainly wouldn't rule him out of what looks a typically open race.'

Both trainer and jockey were increasingly confident about Tiger Roll's chances in the 2m1f test.

That confidence was fully justified, but as Jessica Lamb reported, Cooper was not in the saddle:

Gordon Elliott ended up training him by accident and Davy Russell was in the saddle only because Bryan Cooper suffered a broken right leg after a fall on Wednesday, but Tiger Roll's victory was never in doubt.

Russell, replacing Gigginstown House Stud's retained rider, having himself been replaced by Cooper as the operation's

Opposite page: Tiger Roll makes his debut for trainer Gordon Elliott in the Spring Juvenile Hurdle at Leopardstown in February 2014

1.30 RACE 1

JCB Triumph Hurdle (Grade 1) (Class 1) **CH4**

Winner £68,340   2m1f New

£120,000 guaranteed **For** 4yo **Weights** 11st **Allowances** fillies 7lb **Entries** 65 pay £150 **1st Forfeit** 45 pay £300 **Confirmed** 26 **Penalty value 1st** £68,340 **2nd** £25,644 **3rd** £12,840 **4th** £6,396 **5th** £3,216 **6th** £1,608

1   3111 **ABBYSSIAL** (IRE) [20]   4 11-0   R Walsh (148)
ch g Beneficial-Mega d'Estruval
W P Mullins (IRE)   Mrs Violet O'Leary

2   986 **ACHTUNG** [13]   t 4 11-0   Chris Timmons (98)
b c Montjeu-Funsie
Luke Comer (IRE)   Brian Comer

3   4 **AMORUCCIO** (FR) [21]   4 11-0   James Best (113)
b g Le Fou-Mandchou
Paul Webber   S A Helaissi

4   113314P **BALLYGLASHEEN** (IRE) [2] **CD1**   4 11-0   Adam Wedge (138)
ch g Galileo-Luas Line
Evan Williams   R J Gambarini

5   21 **BROUGHTON** (GER) [40]   4 11-0   Denis O'Regan (147)
b g Teofilo-Boccassini
John Ferguson   Bloomfields

6   211 **CALIPTO** (FR) [34] **D2**   4 11-0   Daryl Jacob (151)
b g Califet-Peutiot
Paul Nicholls   Ian Fogg & Chris Giles

7   F0 **CHERRY TIGER** [8]   4 11-0   Wayne Kavanagh
b g Tiger Hill-Lolla's Spirit
Graeme McPherson   Ms S Howell

8   121211 **GUITAR PETE** (IRE) [33]   v 4 11-0   P Carberry (152)
br g Dark Angel-Innishmore
D T Hughes (IRE)   Mrs P Sloan

9   2-41222 **KENTUCKY HYDEN** (IRE) [48] **D1**   4 11-0   David Bass (149)
ch g Kentucky Dynamite-Cap Serena
Nicky Henderson   Simon Munir & Isaac Souede

10   2121 **LINDENHURST** (IRE) [160] **D1**   t 4 11-0   Mark Bolger (139)
b g Captain Marvelous-Royal Jubilee
John C McConnell (IRE)   Derek Kierans

11   311 **PEARL CASTLE** (IRE) [23] **D2**   4 11-0   Brian Hughes (146)
b g Montjeu-Ghurra
John Quinn   Mr & Mrs Paul Gaffney

12   13 **PLINTH** (IRE) [33]   p 4 11-0   A P McCoy (147)
b g Montjeu-Crazy Volume
A P O'Brien (IRE)   John P McManus

13   1113 **ROYAL IRISH HUSSAR** (IRE) [90] **BF C1 D3**   4 11-0   Barry Geraghty (152)
b c Galileo-Adjalisa
Nicky Henderson   Triermore Stud

14   111 **RUTHERGLEN** (IRE) [72] (29F) **D2**   4 11-0   Noel Fehily (144)
b g Tiger Hill-Hanella
John Quinn   The Beer Swigging Strangers

15   12 **TIGER ROLL** (IRE) [33] **D1**   4 11-0   Davy Russell (150)
b g Authorized-Swiss Roll
Gordon Elliott [2] (IRE)   Gigginstown House Stud

16   8-6312 **ADRIANA DES MOTTES** (FR) [20] **BF**   4 10-7   Paul Townend (147)
br f Network-Daisy Des Mottes
W P Mullins (IRE)   Mrs S Ricci

2013 (17 ran) **Our Conor** D T Hughes 4 11-0 4/1   Bryan Cooper RPR164

BETTING FORECAST: 7-2 Calipto, 6 Broughton, 8 Guitar Pete, Royal Irish Hussar, 9 Pearl Castle, Tiger Roll, 10 Rutherglen, 14 Abbyssial, Plinth, 16 Adriana Des Mottes, Lindenhurst, 25 Kentucky Hyden, 66 Ballyglasheen, 100 Amoruccio, 250 Achtung, Cherry Tiger.

number-one jockey, was to enjoy a day of days, going on to win the Gold Cup two hours later on Lord Windermere and, for good measure and in the same Gigginstown colours, the Grand Annual on Savello.

For Elliott, Tiger Roll's success was a dream come true after a week full of near misses.

Explaining how he came to train the son of 2007 Derby winner Authorized, Elliott revealed: 'I got the horse by accident at the Brightwells sale here in November – there was another horse I wanted the day he was bought and there was a big row on the night.

'They [Gigginstown] told me I could have two other horses instead. These owners are brilliant; Michael and Eddie O'Leary, the whole outfit, are very good to me.'

Elliott's role in the team has changed significantly in the last two seasons. He now produces Gigginstown's point-to-pointers on the condition they then leave his yard.

Yesterday's Albert Bartlett Novices' Hurdle winner Very Wood is one such horse.

Elliott added: 'We've been hitting the crossbar all week and I feel sorry for Bryan Cooper, but I'm delighted for Davy as he's always very lucky when he rides for me.'

Russell sympathised with his successor and said: 'Bryan's young and has plenty of time on his side. He's a good rider and he's tough.'

He added: 'We went a reasonably good gallop over the first and it steadied up after Abbyssial fell, giving us a chance to get back on an even keel.

'Gordon had told me the horse would improve from Leopardstown to here and I had the one who beat him [Guitar Pete] in front of me. I had enough horse left coming off the hill and was confident I'd get there.'

The fall of Abbyssial resulted in a broken arm for Ruby Walsh.

'We don't want to see anybody getting injured,' Russell said. 'But it's only a stride away. That's the line we live on. That's our job, these are the risks we take.'

The winner, who was the first leg of a remarkable four-timer for Gigginstown, who were also on the mark with Don Poli in the Martin Pipe Conditional Jockeys' Handicap Hurdle, is now bound for the Punchestown equivalent and Elliott said: 'This was only his third start over hurdles and I think there's still a bit more improvement.'

RACING POST ANALYSIS – Richard Lowther

This championship event lacked leading juveniles Le Rocher, winner of the Finale Hurdle at Chepstow but ruled out through injury, and Adonis winner Activial, who is being kept for Aintree. It has to rate very much a lesser renewal.

There was drama early on as leader Abbyssial stepped into the second flight and fell heavily, bringing down stablemate Adriana Des Mottes and hampering several others.

Ireland still emerged on top thanks to Tiger Roll, who travelled well into the lead heading down to the last before running on gutsily up the hill. He doesn't have the profile of a typical Triumph winner, having been unraced on the Flat before coming here on the back of just two runs over hurdles, the first of them a winning one for the Nigel Hawke stable at Market Rasen. He's tough and jumps well, and given his lack of experience there could well be more improvement in him. The Champion Four Year Old Hurdle seems a more likely option for him than Aintree's Anniversary Hurdle.

CHELTENHAM
March 14, 2014
JCB Triumph Hurdle
2m1f

1	Tiger Roll	Davy Russell	10-1
2	Kentucky Hyden	David Bass	20-1
3	Guitar Pete	Paul Carberry	7-1

3¼ lengths, 1¾ lengths
15 ran

Russell later reflected on his fantastic afternoon: 'I obviously would have been thrilled with one winner. I was looking forward to Friday. Gordon had given plenty of good vibes about Tiger Roll and every morning I met Jim Culloty he was giving me great confidence. He'd be coming up the chute with Lord Windermere and I'd be going down it on whatever I was riding and every morning he just said, 'I can't wait for Friday, I just can't wait for Friday.'

Nigel Hawke also looked back on Tiger Roll's Triumph Hurdle success and explained what it meant for his own training career.

'Of course there is always the one that got away and mine at the moment is Tiger Roll,' he said.

'But every cloud has a silver lining and the money we made out of the sale has gone towards buying more young horses, which is my way of investing in the future.'

Tiger Roll's season ended disappointingly after he could manage only seventh in the AES Champion Four Year Old Hurdle at the Punchestown festival when starting the 13-8 favourite. The race was won by the Willie Mullins-trained Abbyssial.

Following a summer break Tiger Roll began his second season as a racehorse in the £30,000 Masterson Holdings Hurdle at Cheltenham's opening meeting of the 2014-15 season.

Previous spread: Tiger Roll and Davy Russell come home alone in the Triumph Hurdle

Opposite page, top: Tiger Roll with his jubilant connections after his Triumph Hurdle success

Opposite page, bottom: Eddie O'Leary's wife Wendy greets Tiger Roll in the Cheltenham winner's enclosure

Tiger Roll parades at Fairyhouse's Easter festival in April 2014 three weeks after his Cheltenham triumph

Elliott had high hopes for Tiger Roll, who was as short as 14-1 for that season's Stan James Champion Hurdle on the back of his Triumph Hurdle success, and he fully expected his charge to come on greatly for the run. He got off to a flying start as Andrew King reported:

Tiger Roll made a victorious return to the course when getting the better of a tactical duel for the 2m½f conditions hurdle with Calipto.

The success will also be fondly remembered by jockey Bryan Cooper, as it proved to be a triumphant reappearance on his first ride in Britain since he suffered a broken right leg at the Cheltenham Festival in March.

Cooper said: 'I've had two winners from five rides in Ireland since I came back a couple of weeks ago, and it's good to be on the scoresheet over here again as well.

'I have plenty to look forward to over the coming months with good horses like this one and all the other Gigginstown horses.'

Trainer Gordon Elliott said: 'Tiger Roll wasn't mad about the tacky ground out there but coped with it. He should come on for the run.'

RACING POST ANALYSIS – Ashley Rumney

A high-class contest for last season's juvenile hurdlers and a good finish.

Tiger Roll, a good winner of the Triumph Hurdle here last season, had disappointed on his only subsequent outing. He tracked the leader from the start, but looked in trouble when coming under pressure at the penultimate flight. However, he responded and stuck his head down after the last to gain the advantage up the hill. He has a bit to find with the top hurdlers, but his liking for this track is an advantage.

CHELTENHAM
October 18, 2014
Masterson Holdings Hurdle
2m½f

1	Tiger Roll	Bryan Cooper	15-8
2	Calipto	Sam Twiston-Davies	4-5f
3	Ballyglasheen	Paul Moloney	7-1

½ length, 19 lengths
4 ran

In a Stable Tour following his winning reappearance at Cheltenham, Elliott spoke about the possibility of aiming Tiger Roll at the Champion Hurdle in his first season out of juvenile company.

He said: 'I've never had a Champion Hurdle horse, so I don't know if he's one or not. To give weight to Calipto was a fair performance and he certainly seems to like Cheltenham, which is a great thing. We'll take it one step at a time with him.'

Tiger Roll's next step towards a return to the festival was the Grade 2 WKD Hurdle at Down Royal on October 31, where he faced old rival Guitar Pete as well as the Willie Mullins pair Arctic Fire and Wicklow Brave. However, it was Little King Robin who came out on top to complete a quickfire four-timer. Tiger Roll was pulled up and the vet reported him to be lame post-race.

Elliott hoped that Tiger Roll would have recovered in time to contest the Hatton's Grace Hurdle at Fairyhouse at the end of November, but that race came too soon and instead he returned in the Ryanair Hurdle at Leopardstown's Christmas festival.

A lack of options forced Elliott into running Tiger Roll in the Grade 1 and place money was his best hope against the likes of Hurricane Fly, Jezki and Arctic Fire.

In a thrilling finish dual Champion Hurdle winner Hurricane Fly got the better of Jezki in a no holds barred battle to the line by half a length. It was a 21st Grade 1 success for Hurricane Fly, who was unbeaten at Leopardstown, and the fourth time Willie Mullins' hurdling legend had got the better of the previous season's Champion Hurdle hero. Tiger Roll made a slight mistake at the third-last, after which he found no extra for pressure and was beaten 19 lengths into sixth. It was no disgrace on what was his first run against the best hurdlers in Ireland.

He met the same rivals in the BHP Insurances Irish Champion Hurdle at the end of January 2015 back at Leopardstown, where the outcome was the same as Hurricane Fly claimed yet another top-level victory. This time, though, he beat Arctic Fire by three and a half lengths with Jezki a further four lengths back in third and Tiger Roll in fourth another 11 lengths back.

Tiger Roll was unable to compete against the leading senior hurdlers, so for his next start Elliott tried a new approach. He dropped Tiger Roll into Grade 2 company for the Red Mills Trial Hurdle at Gowran Park in the middle of February and also applied blinkers for the first time. However, it didn't work out as he hoped as Tiger Roll was beaten 18 lengths into third by Kitten Rock.

It was all change again at the Cheltenham Festival as this time Elliott opted to put Tiger Roll up in trip for the Ladbrokes World Hurdle over three miles. He finished down the field, though, as Cole Harden took the honours for Warren Greatrex and Gavin Sheehan.

Tiger Roll ended his season with a tame effort in the Punchestown Champion Hurdle, trailing in last of four runners behind Faugheen, and he didn't reappear until the following spring. He ran on the Flat at Dundalk in March 2016, where he finished runner-up to Sir Raston in a maiden over two miles, before being switched back to hurdles for his final two starts of the season.

At Aintree Tiger Roll had his first taste of Grand National day, but was well beaten in the opening handicap hurdle, while at the Punchestown festival he was pulled up in a 2m4f handicap hurdle.

Although his hurdling career included success at the Cheltenham Festival, Tiger Roll failed to build on that early promise and it was now time for something different.

2
Chasing glory

Previous spread: Tiger Roll and Lisa O'Neill clear the final fence in the National Hunt Chase at Cheltenham in March 2017

Tiger Roll began the next stage of his career in the McHale Fusion 3 Plus Beginners Chase at Ballinrobe in May 2016 just a month after being pulled up over hurdles at the Punchestown festival.

He put in a polished display on his chasing debut under 3lb claimer Jack Kennedy to win going away by eight lengths from 11 rivals, a performance which impressed Gordon Elliott, who said: 'I'm not sure if he can get back to his Triumph Hurdle form but that was good and there is a great programme for this type of horse.'

BALLINROBE

May 31, 2016
McHale Fusion 3 Plus Beginners Chase
2m1f

1	Tiger Roll	Jack Kennedy	5-2jf
2	Buster Dan Dan	David Splaine	11-2
3	Rich Coast	Sean Flanagan	10-1

8 lengths, ½ length
12 ran

RACING POST ANALYSIS – Johnny Ward

Tiger Roll became disappointing after his Triumph Hurdle win but there were positive signs this year and this was a very good performance. He is nimble at his fences – note how he got close into the last but still came away from it really quickly, and it was impressive how he pulled away.

Gordon Elliott watches the action unfold as Tiger Roll makes his second start over fences at Kilbeggan in June 2016

Tiger Roll missed his intended next start two weeks later because of a stone bruise and instead reappeared in the Midlands National Ladies Day July 15th Novice Chase at Kilbeggan. He made it two from two over fences, after which Elliott said: 'That was good – he's been consistent. We'll look at the novice chase in Galway now. He's one of the favourites in the yard. He's had his problems but he's back rocking now.'

Tiger Roll makes it two from two over fences at Kilbeggan with Jack Kennedy in the saddle

RACING POST ANALYSIS – Justin O'Hanlon

Tiger Roll showed a fair bit of class here without looking the most fluent of jumpers. Jack Kennedy was probably glad of these fences being on the soft side as his mount got quite low at one or two, especially the last where he hardly seemed to come up at all. However, he had taken complete command at that stage having travelled nicely to get to the front and having moved clear between the final two fences. He will pay for mistakes like this at one of the better tracks with stiffer fences, but chasing has led to an upsurge in his form and they will hope it continues at Galway.

KILBEGGAN
June 20, 2016
Midlands National Ladies Day July 15th Novice Chase
2m4f

1	Tiger Roll	Jack Kennedy	7-4f
2	Valyssa Monterg	Danny Mullins	7-2
3	Duckweed	Robbie Power	100-30

3½ lengths, 4½ lengths
7 ran

For his next outing Tiger Roll went to Killarney where he finished fourth behind Sandymount Duke. Elliott was pleased with Tiger Roll's progress since the switch to fences and, although he gave him an entry for the prestigious Galway Plate, he instead chose to run him in the novice chase on the Thursday of the big summer festival. It all ended in tears, in particular for Bryan Cooper, as Justin O'Hanlon reported:

Bryan Cooper suffered a partially collapsed lung at Galway yesterday after being unseated from 11-4 favourite Tiger Roll and slammed into the final fence of the 2m2f novice chase.

Further scans were being awaited last night by the Turf Club's chief medical adviser Dr Adrian McGoldrick, who said: 'At the moment he has a partially collapsed lung and we are awaiting a scan report. If that is the extent of his injury he'll be a very lucky fellow.'

Cooper, out of luck on his six rides at the festival this week, has been far from lucky with injuries, having broken his leg twice, including at the 2014 Cheltenham Festival on Clarcam, an injury McGoldrick described as the worst fracture he had ever seen.

With Cooper again on the sidelines, Kennedy took over the ride when Tiger Roll returned three weeks after his mishap at Galway in a 2m4½f novice

Tiger Roll and Bryan Cooper clear a fence before finishing second at Galway in September 2016

chase at Killarney. He finished a length-and-a-half-second to Baily Cloud after being hampered early on.

Cooper had recovered in time for Tiger Roll's next run at Galway in early September as David Jennings reported:

Not only does Bryan Cooper return to the scene of the crime today, he is riding the horse who committed the crime.

Tiger Roll left Cooper with a laceration of his liver and a partially collapsed lung after he sent him crashing into the take-off board of the final fence following a mistake at the second-last in a novice chase at Galway in July, and the pair are back over the same course and distance in search of better luck in the feature Grade 3 Ballybrit Novice Chase.

'I suppose it is a bit ironic all right,' said the jockey. 'To be riding the horse who injured you on your first ride back from the injury is probably something that's never happened before, but I'm not one bit worried about it.

'Up until that mistake Tiger Roll has been deadly over his fences – and he has since run well at Killarney – and it was just a freak accident.

'I suppose when I saw the entries the other day I knew it might happen as I knew I'd be unable to do the weight on the filly [Tocororo].'

He added: 'You can't be thinking about things like falls and injuries when you go out to ride a horse. The blinkers are on this time and I think Tiger Roll has a big chance. Fingers crossed he can give me a winner on my return.'

There was no such drama this time for Cooper, but there was the frustration of having to gaze in the distance at the other Gigginstown runner Tocororo as the pair finished a 16-length second to Kennedy's mount, with Elliott saddling the first two home. Just 11 days later Tiger Roll finished second again at Listowel.

Cooper's tale of injury woe continued at Fairyhouse at the start of October as the rider was rushed to Connolly Hospital in Blanchardstown for X-rays on a suspected broken arm following a first-fence fall from odds-on favourite Ball D'Arc in a 2m beginners' chase.

This meant the ride on Tiger Roll in the Munster National at Limerick in October was up for grabs, with initially Lisa O'Neill inked in for the mount, but it was Donagh Meyler who stepped in as David Jennings reported:

Gordon Elliott picked Limerick as the stage for his latest Paul Daniels impression as he turned the 2014 Triumph Hurdle winner into a Munster National winner.

Bryan Cooper has ridden Tiger Roll 13 times

Tiger Roll puts in a magnificent leap on the way to winning the JT McNamara Munster National at Limerick under Donagh Meyler in October 2016

This magic trick was all the more mesmerising when you take into consideration that Tiger Roll looked about as enthusiastic as a child heading to the dentist when well beaten in a novice chase at Listowel last month.

So remote did Elliott think his chances were that he phoned Eddie O'Leary, of owners Gigginstown House Stud, to discuss taking him out and running at Punchestown on Thursday instead.

Lisa O'Neill even jumped ship and hopped back on board her Kerry National winner Wrath Of Titans after Gigginstown's number-one jockey Bryan Cooper broke his arm.

Donagh Meyler stepped in, just as he had on Lord Scoundrel in the Galway Plate in July, and the outcome was the same as the 20-1 shot strolled to a seven-length success from Stellar Notion in a contest now run as the JT McNamara Ladbrokes Munster National, following the death of the popular jockey in July.

'I didn't want to run him, I wanted to take him out this morning,' confessed Elliott.

'All the credit has to go to Eddie. I was mad keen to take him out because of the ground, but then it dried and he wanted him to run. He was right and I was wrong. Fair play to him.'

Sparing a thought for O'Neill, he added: 'Poor Lisa! I took her off him this morning but she wanted to ride Wrath Of Titans again and wouldn't swap him. It's great for Donagh to come in and do what he did.

'It's great to win the race, especially now since it's in John Thomas's name as I'd been friends with him since we were little nippers in school. That made it extra special.'

It was extra special for Meyler too as he once again proved he is the most able of deputies when called on by Gigginstown and Elliott.

'He gave me a great spin, jumped great and travelled into the race very well,' said the 20-year-old from Kilmacow, in County Kilkenny.

'On the first circuit he was travelling away, which he probably doesn't do normally.

'He was travelling strongly in my hands and carrying me down to the fences and coming down to the last, when I took a look around, I really couldn't believe I was so far in front. I had to have two glances to make sure.'

It was another National for Elliott, swiftly following his Kerry one last month – also for Gigginstown, who are farming staying handicap chases on both sides of the Irish Sea. So can he become champion trainer in Ireland? 'I doubt it,' he replied. 'Willie Mullins is the man. I know that and everyone else knows that.'

Left: Caroline McNamara (right) joins Tiger Roll and his connections in the Limerick winner's enclosure

Right: Tiger Roll and Donagh Meyler are led in after the Munster National

Mullins might be the man at the moment, but if Elliott keeps pulling rabbits out of the hat like this one he will have a fight on his hands to keep his title.

LIMERICK

October 9, 2016

JT McNamara Ladbrokes Munster National Handicap Chase

3m

1	Tiger Roll	Donagh Meyler	20-1
2	Stellar Notion	David Mullins	13-2
3	Kylecrue	Danny Mullins	12-1

7 lengths, 3¼ lengths

15 ran

RACING POST ANALYSIS – David Jennings

Tiger Roll did not jump off the page beforehand. He looked anything but enthusiastic about being asked to jump fences at Listowel last month where everything was an effort and Bryan Cooper earned every cent of his riding fee. It was a different story here. We knew he had the ability, he wouldn't have won a Triumph Hurdle otherwise, but he did not look to be crying out for the helter-skelter of a 3m handicap chase.

He loved it, though, and won his first handicap over fences with plenty up his sleeve. His jumping was good, albeit a bit slow at times, and he never looked in danger from a mile out. He needs decent ground, so the Paddy Power at Leopardstown might be out. Whether he can back up this display with a similar one is anyone's guess.

More than two and a half years after winning the Triumph Hurdle it seemed as though Tiger Roll had started to turn a corner – it was as if a switch had been flicked inside his head. He was finally consenting to show the ability he clearly possessed.

'We were thrilled with the way he won the Munster National,' Elliott said before Tiger Roll's next race at Cheltenham's first meeting of the season. 'He surprised me there, but as a Triumph Hurdle winner he's always had ability. The ground will suit and he's been in good form since Limerick.'

Tiger Roll finished third at Cheltenham under leading amateur Jamie Codd and had one more run before a winter break. He was third again, this time at Wexford, and in the spring a fresh target had entered connections' thinking – the Grand National. However, that wouldn't happen in 2017 as David Carr reported:

Gigginstown's withdrawal of a controversially handicapped trio of Randox Health Grand National entries has helped clear the way for Aintree veterans Highland Lodge and Vics Canvas.

Michael O'Leary had a war of words with BHA handicapper Phil Smith over his treatment of Outlander, Empire Of Dirt and Don Poli, three of the original four topweights, and has lived up to his vow to take all three out at the first scratchings deadline.

Opposite page: Tiger Roll on the gallops at Cullentra House Stables in February 2017

4.50
RACE 6

JT McNamara National Hunt
Challenge Cup Amateur Riders' Novices'
Chase (Grade 2) (Class 1)
Winner £71,952   (3m 7f 170y)**4m Old**

RUK

£120,000 guaranteed **For** 5yo+ **Weights** 5yo 11st 4lb; 6yo+ 11st 6lb **Weight for age** 5 from 6yo+ 1lb
Allowances mares 7lb **Entries** 26 pay £150 **1st Forfeit** 41 pay £300 **2nd Forfeit** 26 pay £150 **Penalty value**
1st £71,952 **2nd** £22,476 **3rd** £11,232 **4th** £5,616 **5th** £2,808 **6th** £1,416

1	1-63212	**A GENIE IN ABOTTLE** (IRE) 45 **BF**	6 11-6	Mr J J Codd
		b g Beneficial-Erkindale Miss		(154)
		Noel Meade (IRE) Gigginstown House Stud		
2	203-022	**ARBRE DE VIE** (FR) 52 **BF**	7 11-6	Ms K Walsh
		b g Antarctique-Nouvelle Recrue		(158)
		W P Mullins (IRE) Mrs S Ricci		
3	9-51234	**ARPEGE D'ALENE** (FR) 24 **BF**	tb 7 11-6	Mr W Biddick
		gr g Dom Alco-Joliette d'Alene		(159)
		Paul Nicholls Mr&mrs P K Barber,G Mason,Sir A Ferguson		
4	0-2343P	**BALLYCROSS** 59	6 11-6	Mr H F Nugent
		b g King's Theatre-Ninna Nanna		(148)
		Nigel Twiston-Davies The Autism Rockers		
5	40-0711	**BELLS 'N' BANJOS** (IRE) 41	7 11-6	Miss A E Stirling
		b g Indian River-Beechill Dancer		(146)
		Fergal O'Brien The Maple Hurst Partnership		
6	431-111	**BEWARE THE BEAR** (IRE) 90	7 11-6	Mr S Waley-Cohen
		b g Shantou-Native Bid		(161)
		Nicky Henderson G B Barlow		
7	-P312S1	**BIGBADJOHN** (IRE) 24	8 11-6	Mr Barry O'Neill
		br g Vinnie Roe-Celtic Serenade		(156)
		Rebecca Curtis Nigel Morris		
8	133-126	**CHAMPERS ON ICE** (IRE) 45 **BF** C1	tp1 7 11-6	Mr R P Quinlan
		gr g Robin Des Champs-Miss Nova		(156)
		David Pipe Professor Caroline Tisdall & Bryan Drew		
9	-362411	**DANCING SHADOW** (IRE) 38	p 8 11-6	Mr Sean Houlihan
		br g Craigsteel-Be My Shadow		(151)
		Victor Dartnall The Dancing Shadows		
10	-3U21F1	**EDWULF** 16	t 8 11-6	Mr Derek O'Connor
		b g Kayf Tara-Valentines Lady		(165)
		Joseph Patrick O'Brien (IRE) John P McManus		
11	P010-42	**FLINTHAM** 24	p 8 11-6	Mr M Legg
		b g Kayf Tara-Plaid Maid		(151)
		Mark Bradstock The Rasher Partnership		
12	4-51243	**HAYMOUNT** (IRE) 23	8 11-6	Mr P W Mullins
		ch g Presenting-Ali's Dipper		(152)
		W P Mullins (IRE) Mrs C M Hurley		
13	2-F1612	**KERROW** (IRE) 46	7 11-6	Mr Joshua Newman
		b g Mahler-Olives Hall		(148)
		Alan King Trevor Hemmings		
14	37-2145	**MARTELLO TOWER** (IRE) 45 C1	b1 9 11-6	Mr S Clements
		b g Milan-Johnsalice		(149)
		Ms Margaret Mullins (IRE) Barry Connell		
15	P2-413U	**MISSED APPROACH** (IRE) 17 **BF**	p1 7 11-6	Mr N McParlan
		b g Golan-Polly's Dream		(157)
		Warren Greatrex Alan & Andrew Turner		
16	U222133	**TIGER ROLL** (IRE) 134 C2	tb 7 11-6	Ms L O'Neill
		b g Authorized-Swiss Roll		(159)
		Gordon Elliott (IRE) Gigginstown House Stud		
17	-22155P	**WHAT A MOMENT** (IRE) 41 C1	p 7 11-6	Mr R O Harding
		b g Milan-Cuiloge Lady		(146)
		David Pipe Bryan Drew & Steve Roper		
18	43-1212	**CALETT MAD** (FR) 38	t 5 11-4	Mr Z Baker
		b/br g Axxos-Omelia		(157)
		Nigel Twiston-Davies Simon Munir & Isaac Souede		

2016 (20 ran) Minella Rocco Jonjo O'Neill 6 11-6 8/1   Mr Derek O'Connor RPR160

BETTING FORECAST: 9-2 A Genie In Abottle, 5 Edwulf, 8 Beware The Bear,
Champers On Ice, 11 Arpege d'Alene, 12 Bigbadjohn, Martello Tower,
16 Haymount, Tiger Roll, 20 Arbre de Vie, Flintham, 25 Calett Mad, Dancing
Shadow, Missed Approach, 33 Kerrow, 40 bar.

Gigginstown withdrew eight horses in all – the others were Clarcam, Devils Bride, Tiger Roll, A Toi Phil and The Game Changer – and are now quoted at 25-1 (from 20) by Betway to repeat last year's win in the race.

Tiger Roll was now all set for a return to the Cheltenham Festival where, three years after winning over 2m1f, he would face the challenge of the meeting's longest trip in the National Hunt Chase. The marathon four-mile distance is an unknown for many novice chasers, but Elliott was confident of a good performance as he reported that Tiger Roll was 'working like a bomb' in the run-up to the race.

That confidence wasn't misplaced as James Burn explained:

It was not quite turning water into wine, or lead into gold, but as transformations go turning a Flat-bred Triumph Hurdle winner into a horse with enough stamina to power up the hill and land the festival's longest race takes some doing. But Gordon Elliott can do little wrong and Tiger Roll provided him with the last leg of a memorable first-day 1,988-1 treble.

A Darley cast-off, Tiger Roll won the Triumph Hurdle in 2014 and was also completing a fine day for owner Michael O'Leary, whose Gigginstown House Stud operation won the Mares' Hurdle with the Elliott-trained Apple's Jade.

And to complete a magical set, the son of Authorized was giving Lisa O'Neill, who helps Elliott in the office, a first festival winner from her first ride.

After being congratulated by Sir Alex Ferguson, part-owner of fourth-placed Arpege D'Alene, O'Leary said: 'That was some performance after winning the Triumph to win the four-miler. Lisa's a great rider and won the Kerry National for us on Wrath Of Titans.

'She works in the office with Gordon and is a brilliant pilot; it was a great ride. He really enjoyed her and just rolled along.'

The race was run in honour of ace amateur JT McNamara, paralysed after a festival fall in 2013 and who died last year, and Tiger Roll was victorious in October's Munster National, which also carried the late rider's name.

'Everyone misses JT and he bestrode this place,' added O'Leary. 'It's an honour to win a race named after him.'

Echoing that view, O'Neill said: 'JT was an icon to all of us in the point-to-point world and it's a privilege to win this race.'

She continued: 'Tiger Roll is a brilliant horse to have at home and he loved it today. He was a bit free with me early on and I was

Top: Lisa O'Neill sits tight on Tiger Roll in the National Hunt Chase

Bottom: Tiger Roll and Lisa O'Neill return after victory in the National Hunt Chase

wondering whether he'd finish it out, but he did. I think he was taking the mickey out of me because he was loving it so much.

'I'm a bit of a pessimist so I never count my eggs until they're hatched. Today's a great day, I'll really enjoy it.'

While O'Neill, 30, was beaming from ear to ear and O'Leary, boss of airline Ryanair, was walking on cloud nine, so much so he threatened to fly home after racing – 'it doesn't get any better than this' – Elliott was more grounded after capturing his third National Hunt Chase.

'I'm very lucky to have some brilliant staff and horses, and it's a great day,' he said.

The trainer, whose treble was initiated by Supreme winner Labaik, said he would point Tiger Roll at the BoyleSports Irish Grand National at Fairyhouse on April 17.

RACING POST ANALYSIS – Dave Orton

Tiger Roll took this apart under a positive ride and the 2014 Triumph Hurdle winner provided Gordon Elliott with an opening-day treble. His pilot deserves plenty of credit as he's only small and she got him into a great rhythm, the pair overcoming one notable blunder. This going was right up his street and it was probably a return to the level that saw him hose up in last year's Munster National at Limerick. He now heads for the Irish National next month.

CHELTENHAM
March 14, 2017
JT McNamara National Hunt Challenge Cup
Amateur Riders' Novices' Chase
4m

1	Tiger Roll	Lisa O'Neill	16-1
2	Missed Approach	Noel McParlan	50-1
3	Haymount	Patrick Mullins	33-1

3 lengths, ¾ length
18 ran

Tiger Roll ran in the Irish Grand National at Fairyhouse, but was pulled up having bled during the race. It was a disappointing end to a campaign which had brought Tiger Roll notable success at home in the Munster National and on the biggest stage in jump racing, the Cheltenham Festival. It was a marked improvement on the previous season and showed just how good a racehorse he really was.

3
New approach

Previous spread: Racegoers watch on as
Tiger Roll clears the final obstacle in the Cross
Country Chase at Cheltenham in March 2018

Tiger Roll was now an established name in the world of jump racing courtesy of his two victories at the Cheltenham Festival and, although the 2017-18 season would bring even greater recognition, he began the year in unconventional fashion when lining up for the John Shortt Legends Challenge race at Punchestown in October.

The one-mile-six-furlong Flat contest, which involved many big-name riders of the past including Mick Kinane, Paul Carberry and Charlie Swan, was organised to raise funds for the family of John Shortt, the former jump jockey who lost his battle with cancer in February 2017, aged 53.

Tiger Roll makes a splash at Cullentra House
Stables in October 2017

Tiger Roll finished an eight-and-a-half-length second to stablemate Pallasator, a satisfactory warm-up for his return over fences at Wexford 11 days later. Elliott said before that race: 'He's a stable star and is in very good form. The ground might not be ideal for him, but if he runs a nice race I'd be very happy.'

Tiger Roll ran a cracker to finish second to odds-on favourite A Genie In Abottle by a length a half conceding 6lb to the winner.

Two and a half weeks later Tiger Roll was joined by three other Gigginstown runners in the Clonmel Oil Chase as the owners sought a fourth win in the race. Elliott said beforehand that the 2m4½f trip would be on the short side for Tiger Roll, and he was tailed off when pulled up after the third-last fence under Keith Donoghue, who was on board for the first time.

Tiger Roll then tackled Cheltenham's cross-country course for the first time at the December meeting, but could finish only fifth behind Bless The Wings. He promised to get closer before a blunder at the 27th obstacle halted his momentum.

In the spring, as thoughts turned to Cheltenham and the spring festivals, Gigginstown again blasted the BHA over its framing of the weights for the Grand National the previous year.

Tiger Roll (far side) finishes second to stablemate and fellow Gigginstown-owned A Genie In Abottle at Wexford in October 2017

Eddie O'Leary, racing manager for
Gigginstown House Stud

Michael O'Leary said: 'It's a race we love and we'll always have runners in it as long as they aren't handicapped out of the thing.'

The weights for the 2018 running were revealed in mid-February as Tony O'Hehir reported:

Gigginstown have 11 entries for the Randox Health Grand National with six of them – Outlander, Sub Lieutenant, Valseur Lido, Alpha Des Obeaux, Tiger Roll and A Genie In Abottle – in the top 40 and therefore guaranteed a run.

Triple Grade 1-winning chaser Outlander is the highest-weighted of the 11 with 11st 8lb and, according to Eddie O'Leary, the Gordon Elliott-trained ten-year-old might be Aintree bound but not for the National.

O'Leary said: 'If Outlander goes to Aintree it's much more likely he'll run in the Bowl and not the National.

'It's early days yet but looking at our entries I'd pick out Alpha Des Obeaux, Tiger Roll and A Genie In Abottle as three who could well take their chance in the National.

'We'll wait and see. Many of our entries will probably run again before Aintree and we'll review things as we go along.'

The Elliott-trained Tiger Roll, a dual Cheltenham Festival winner who landed the National Hunt Chase last year and who also has a Munster National on his CV, is likely to run in the Glenfarclas Cross Country Chase next month.

Elliott brought Tiger Roll over to Cheltenham to school over the cross-country course and he said: 'He's been brilliant for us and I think he'll run well again this year.'

On the eve of Cheltenham Lisa O'Neill recalled the memorable day for the Elliott team 12 months earlier when she rode Tiger Roll to victory in the National Hunt Chase:

I had just pulled on the maroon-and-white silks of Gigginstown House Stud before fixing my gaze at one of the televisions in the weigh room where I watched Apple's Jade win the Mares' Hurdle from Vroum Vroum Mag and Limini.

I got a few funny looks from some of the jockeys in there because I shouted the house down when she came home in front.

Tiger Roll was my ride in the following race, the National Hunt Chase, and I went out into the parade ring absolutely buzzing after the race because Apple's Jade is one of my favourite horses in Gordon's.

Everyone always says it, but working for Gordon is like being a part of a big team, and after Jack's [Kennedy] first festival win on Labaik in the Supreme, the Mares' Hurdle win with Apple's Jade and then for me to win the National Hunt Chase was probably one of the standout days I've ever experienced in racing – a treble on day one of the festival!

Georgie Benson looks after Apple's Jade, and she says just how professional a racemare she is. I'm lucky enough that I get to ride her every day and she's just a dream to have anything to do with.

It's hard to believe that she's only a six-year-old and all that she's achieved already but she really showed the world how tough she was in winning that Mares' Hurdle.

Did it give me confidence going out to ride in the race afterwards? Definitely. I can remember talking to Gordon before I got the leg-up on Tiger Roll and everyone was still buzzing after Apple's Jade. We could almost do no wrong. There was obviously pressure on me but I didn't feel it. What a day!

Tom Kerr witnessed a sparkling performance from Tiger Roll:

A year after announcing he would take a break from riding due to weight issues, a decision which cost him a first Cheltenham Festival victory on Labaik, Keith Donoghue made amends by guiding the plucky Tiger Roll to Cross Country glory.

Donoghue, 24, who returned to the saddle in May last year, wages an unceasing battle with the scales and runs countless miles to keep the pounds off, but the constant sacrifice was worth it for what the jockey called 'the best feeling in the world'.

He said: 'I lost 8lb to ride this horse because my weight hasn't been great recently. It's worth it. It's a dream come true after last year, missing the winner on Labaik was very hard to take. This might not be a Grade 1 but it's every bit as good to me.

'I've given up three or four times because of my weight, but Gordon [Elliott] always pulls me back and gives me rides when I can do the weight. If it wasn't for Gordon I wouldn't be standing here. This day last year I was 12st 7lb; here I'm riding off 11st 2lb.'

Tiger Roll has become something of a cult hero among the Cheltenham crowd, who have now seen him win three different races at the festival.

Those races could scarcely be a less likely treble – being the two-mile Triumph Hurdle in 2014, the four-mile National Hunt Chase last year, and now the idiosyncratic Cross Country – but Tiger Roll

Lisa O'Neill has nothing but happy memories of her victory on Tiger Roll in the 2017 National Hunt Chase

4.10
RACE 5

Glenfarclas Chase (A Cross Country Chase) (Class 2)
Winner £40,235 (3m 6f 37y) **3m6f X-Country**

ITV

£65,000 guaranteed **For** 5yo+ **Weights** 5yo 11st 2lb; 6yo+ 11st 4lb **Allowances** mares 7lb **Entries** 20 pay £90 **Confirmed** 20 pay £235.00 **Penalty value 1st** £40,235 **2nd** £11,947 **3rd** £5,973.50 **4th** £2,977 **5th** £1,495 **6th** £754 **7th** £377 **8th** £182

1	-12B3F1 **AUVERGNAT** (FR) [31] S6	8 11-4	
	b g Della Francesca-Hesmeralda	Mark Walsh	158
	E Bolger (IRE) John P McManus		
2	5511-19 **BEEVES** (IRE) [283] (38H) S3 F1	b 11 11-4	
	b g Portrait Gallery-Camas North	Sean Quinlan	162
	Jennie Candlish Paul & Clare Rooney		
3	226-PP1 **BLESS THE WINGS** (IRE) [89] S1 C1 CD1	p 13 11-4	
	b g Winged Love-Silva Venture	Davy Russell	162
	Gordon Elliott (IRE) Adrian Butler/S P O'Connor		
4	232-042 **CANTLOW** (IRE) [89] S3 F1 CD1	p 13 11-4	
	b g Kayf Tara-Winnowing	Donal McInerney	160
	E Bolger (IRE) John P McManus		
5	P0512-0 **CAUSE OF CAUSES** (USA) [38] S3 C2 CD1	tp 10 11-4	
	b g Dynaformer-Angel In My Heart	Mr J J Codd	168
	Gordon Elliott (IRE) John P McManus		
6	34417-3 **CHIC NAME** (FR) [31]	h 6 11-4	
	b g Nickname-Vuelta Al Ruedo	Jonathan Burke	146
	Richard Hobson The Boom Syndicate		
7	-514553 **FEDERICI** [21] S3	p 9 11-4	
	b g Overbury-Vado Via	Will Kennedy	146
	Donald McCain Jon Glews		
8	-401104 **HURRICANE DARWIN** (IRE) [31] S2	t 8 11-4	
	b g Westerner-Poetics Girl	Denis O'Regan	144
	Alan Fleming (IRE) Barry Connell		
9	0-62302 **JOSIES ORDERS** (IRE) [31] S2 CD3	p 10 11-4	
	b g Milan-Silent Orders	Ms N Carberry	160
	E Bolger (IRE) John P McManus		
10	53F23-P **SAINT ARE** (FR) [340] (46H)	tp 12 11-4	
	b/br g Network-Fortanea	A P Heskin	161
	Tom George D W Fox		
11	320-224 **THE LAST SAMURI** (IRE) [46] S5	10 11-4	
	ch g Flemensfirth-Howaboutthis	David Bass	173
	Kim Bailey Paul & Clare Rooney		
12	31P-2P5 **TIGER ROLL** (IRE) [89] S1 C3	tp 8 11-4	
	b g Authorized-Swiss Roll	Keith Donoghue	165
	Gordon Elliott (IRE) Gigginstown House Stud		
13	7351-23 **URGENT DE GREGAINE** (FR) [117] S1 F1 CD1	tp 10 11-4	
	b g Truth Or Dare I-Hispanie	Felix de Giles	157
	Emmanuel Clayeux (FR) Arnaud Rasquier		
14	3-13P22 **URUMQI** (FR) [24] S2	t1 7 11-4	
	b g Soldier Of Fortune-Love In Paradise	Jonathan Plouganou	140
	D Cottin (FR) Ecurie De Roebeck		
15	1481312 **VICOMTE DU SEUIL** (FR) [117] S7	tp 9 11-4	
	b g Special Kaldoun-Marie Du Seuil	Charlie Deutsch	149
	Emmanuel Clayeux (FR) Mrs M Boudot		
16	-F63327 **BELAMIX DOR** (FR) [40]	t1 7 10-11	
	b m Al Namix-Paladoune	Thomas Beaurain	136
	Patrice Quinton (FR) Ecurie Du Haras D'Erable		

2017 (16 ran) Cause Of Causes Gordon Elliott 9 11-4 4/1   Mr J J Codd RPR158

BETTING FORECAST: 11-4 Cause Of Causes, 5 Tiger Roll, 11-2 The Last Samuri, 6 Josies Orders, 7 Auvergnat, 9 Bless The Wings, 14 Urgent de Gregaine, 20 Cantlow, 25 Hurricane Darwin, 33 Beeves, Saint Are, Vicomte Du Seuil, 40 Federici, Urumqi, 50 Belamix Dor, 66 Chic Name.

Tiger Roll and Keith Donoghue (second left) clear the cheese wedges as they track the leaders in the Cross Country Chase

continues to defy his diminutive size and seems to relish whatever challenge is thrown at him.

'The secret to him seems to be there's no distance too far – the further he goes the better he is,' said Michael O'Leary of owners Gigginstown.

'I thought he had no chance because he's really a good-ground horse. He's only small, he's a little rat of a thing, but he's got a heart of a lion.'

Tiger Roll took it up five out and was travelling the best of the small band who saw out the three miles six furlongs in stamina-sapping conditions, although French raider Urgent De Gregaine more than justified the trip over by emerging much the best of the rest as a two-length runner-up, with Aintree-bound The Last Samuri running a fine National prep in third.

'You watch these things and you see the battalions of McManus horses and Enda Bolger horses coming and you think, 'Ah well, you know we had a nice run and then JP wins,' added O'Leary. 'I'm just surprised and delighted, especially delighted for Keith and delighted for Gordon and all the team.'

RACING POST ANALYSIS – David Toft

Tiger Roll, who won the National Hunt Challenge Cup last year, finished well behind a few of these over course and distance in December but, after travelling really strongly close up, was never going to stop once gaining a nice advantage and always seemed likely to hang on. It's quite amazing to think his first success at this festival came in the 2014 Triumph Hurdle and jockey Keith Donoghue reported after today's win that he'd battled hard to lose 8lb to be able to take the ride. The gelding is in both the Irish and Aintree Nationals, so has a couple of nice options for the remainder of the season. One For Arthur (officially rated 148 that day) proved eight-year-olds can land the latter race last season and, judged on this performance, Gordon Elliott's horse would be a great ride there.

CHELTENHAM
March 14, 2018
Glenfarclas Chase (A Cross Country Chase)
3m6f

1	Tiger Roll	Keith Donoghue	7-1
2	Urgent De Gregaine	Felix de Giles	12-1
3	The Last Samuri	David Bass	11-4f

2 lengths, 11 lengths
16 ran

Having conquered the Cheltenham Festival three times in three different races in three different disciplines, it was now time for a new test – the Grand National – and, having taken so well to the cross-country race, it gave hope that the spruce fences might be just the type of challenge Tiger Roll would relish.

51

4
National
success

Previous spread: Tiger Roll gets his head in front where it matters from Pleasant Company in the Grand National at Aintree in April 2018

G ordon Elliott had, of course, already created his own slice of Grand National history in 2007 with Silver Birch, so he knew what it took to win the great race. Gigginstown House Stud had also tasted success in the Aintree spectacular with Rule The World in 2016.

In 2017 Cause Of Causes finished second to One For Arthur for Elliott, so he was also a candidate for the race, but his trainer reported he was stiff and sore after being pulled up behind Tiger Roll in the Cross Country Chase at Cheltenham.

Of Tiger Roll, Elliott said: 'He's come out of Cheltenham well and the Grand National is the plan for him.'

However, there would be disappointment for Keith Donoghue as he wouldn't be able to ride Tiger Roll at Aintree because he would be unable to do the required weight of 10st 13lb. He remained positive about the eight-year-old's chances though.

The jockeys pose for their traditional photo in the parade ring before the Grand National

5.15 RACE 6
Randox Health Grand National
Handicap Chase (Class 1) (Grade 3) Winner £500,000

ITV

Tote Scoop6: Leg 5

Going: HEAVY (Soft in places)

4m2½f (4m2f74y)

£1,000,000 guaranteed For 7yo+ rated 125 or more. Highest weight 11st10lb Minimum weight 10st Blaklion's Handicap Mark 161
Entries 105 pay £1,700 1st Forfeit 90 pay £1,100 2nd Forfeit 73 pay £1,100 Confirmed 63 pay £1,700. Penalty value 1st £500,000
2nd £200,000 3rd £100,000 4th £65,000 5th £40,000 6th £30,000 7th £20,000 8th £15,000, 9th £10,000, 10th £5,000

No	Form	Horse	Jockey	Wgt
1	-P84PFF	THUNDER AND ROSES (IRE) 12 S5 — b/br g Presenting-Glen Empress — M F Morris (IRE) Gigginstown House Stud	tp J J Slevin	10 10-5 (172)
2	324-212	BLAKLION 56 BF S5 C1 — b g Kayf Tara-Franciscaine — Nigel Twiston-Davies S Such & CG Paletta	w¹ Sam Twiston-Davies	9 11-10 (171)
3	2-591F3	ANIBALE FLY (FR) 29 S5 — b g Assessor-Nouba Fly — A J Martin (IRE) John P McManus	t8 Barry Geraghty	11-8 (177)
4	20-2243	THE LAST SAMURI (IRE) 31 BF S5 — ch g Flemensfirth-Howaboutthis — Kim Bailey Paul & Clare Rooney	t¹ David Bass	10 11-8 (170)
5	14-5553	VALSEUR LIDO (FR) 16 BF S5 — b g Anzillero-Libido Rock — Henry de Bromhead (IRE) Gigginstown House Stud	9 ¹Keith Donoghue	11-7 (173)
6	05-111F	TOTAL RECALL (IRE) 29 S5 — b g Westerner-August Weekend — W P Mullins (IRE) Slaneyville Syndicate	9 Paul Townend	11-5 (170)
7	2414646	ALPHA DES OBEAUX (FR) 69 S2 — b g Saddler Maker-Omega Des Obeaux — M F Morris (IRE) Gigginstown House Stud	p8 Rachael Blackmore	11-4 (172)
8	1P-0105	PERFECT CANDIDATE (IRE) 77 S5 — b g Winged Love-Dansana — Fergal O'Brien ISL Recruitment	11 Alain Cawley	11-3 (172)
9	5PP2222	SHANTOU FLYER (IRE) 32 S2 — b g Shantou-Carrigmorna Flyer — Richard Hobson Carl Hinchy	tv 8 James Bowen	11-2 (172)
10	3120-P6	TENOR NIVERNAIS (FR) 56 S7 — b g Shaanmer-Hosanna II — Venetia Williams Boultbee Brooks Ltd	11 ¹Tom O'Brien	11-1 (172)
11	44-7U5P	CARLINGFORD LOUGH (IRE) 107 S5 — b g King's Theatre-Baden — John E Kiely (IRE) John P McManus	12 Mark Walsh	11-1 (172)
12	-331353	DELUSIONOFGRANDEUR (IRE) 14 S2 — b g Mahler-Olivia Rose — Sue Smith Mcgoldrick Racing 3	8 Henry Brooke	10-5 (172)
13	1P-2P51	TIGER ROLL (IRE) 31 S2 — b g Authorized-Swiss Roll — Gordon Elliott (IRE) Gigginstown House Stud	tp 8 Davy Russell	10-11 (177)
14	P8-03P1	REGAL ENCORE (IRE) 56 S2 — b g King's Theatre-Go On Eileen — Anthony Honeyball John P McManus	10 Richie McLernon	10-13 (172)
15	116-474	VIEUX LION ROUGE (FR) 56 S7 C1 — ch g Sabiango-Indecise — David Pipe Prof Caroline Tisdall & John Gent	p 9 Tom Scudamore	10-13 (176)
16	751-1PP	CHASE THE SPUD 49 B1 S4 — b g Alflora-Trial Trip — Fergal O'Brien Mrs C Banks	Paddy Brennan	10-11 (168)
17	115-U22	WARRIORS TALE 77 S2 F1 — b g Midnight Legend-Samandara — Paul Nicholls Trevor Hemmings	t9 Sean Bowen	10-11 (171)
18	3/1P2-3	SEEYOUATMIDNIGHT 21 S5 — b g Midnight Legend-Morsky Baloo — Sandy Thomson Mrs David Thompson	w² Brian Hughes	10 10-11 (175)
19	445-F13	GAS LINE BOY (IRE) 96 S2 C1 — b g Blueprint-Jervia — Ian Williams The Three Graces	v 12 Robert Dunne	10-11 (172)
20	27-261P	THE DUTCHMAN (IRE) 56 S2 — b g King's Theatre-Shivertimber — Colin Tizzard Sprayclad UK	t8 Harry Cobden	10-11 (172)
21	1419-0P	PLEASANT COMPANY (IRE) 79 S2 — b g Presenting-Katie Flame — W P Mullins (IRE) Malcolm C Denmark	10 David Mullins	10-11 (168)
22	724U-2P	UCELLO CONTI (FR) 79 S3 F2 — gr g Martaline-Gazelle Lulu — Gordon Elliott (IRE) Simon Munir & Isaac Souede	t10 Daryl Jacob	10-10 (172)
23	3F23-PP	SAINT ARE (FR) 31 — b/br g Network-Fontanea — Tom George D W Fox	tb A P Heskin	12 10-10 (170)
24	97-513P	WALK IN THE MILL (FR) 84 S3 — b g Walk In The Park-Libre Amour — Robert Walford Baroness Harding	¹Mr Sam Waley-Cohen	8 10-4 (174)
25	P0-F221	RAZ DE MAREE (FR) 96 S5 — ch g Shaanmer-Diyala III — Gavin Cromwell (IRE) James J Swan	13 ¹Robbie Power	10-9 (175)
26	P3-3412	I JUST KNOW 93 (28H) BF S3 — b g Robin Des Pres-Desperado Queen — Sue Smith M B Scholey & The Late R H Scholey	8 Danny Cook	10-8 (169)
27	223-18P	VIRGILIO 119 S3 — b g Denham Red-Liesse de Marbeuf — Dan Skelton C J Edwards, D Futter, A H Rushworth	w¹ 19 Harry Skelton	10-8 (174)
28	513-663	BAIE DES ILES (FR) 62 S6 — gr m Barastraight-Malownia — Ross O'Sullivan (IRE) Mrs Z Wentworth	p 7 Ms K Walsh	10-8 (169)
29	504-443	MAGGIO (FR) 26 S1 — b g Trempolino-La Musardiere — Patrick Griffin (IRE) D G Pryde/James Beaumont	t13 ¹Brendan Powell	10-8 (163)
30	150/2-0	PENDRA (IRE) 30 S3 — ch g Old Vic-Mariah Rollins — Charlie Longsdon John P McManus	w¹ tb Aidan Coleman	10 10-8 (171)
31	04-8610	BUYWISE (IRE) 98 (70H) S5 — b g Tikkanen-Greenogue Princess — Evan Williams T Hywel Jones	Adam Wedge	8 10-8 (168)
32	/951-2P	CHILDRENS LIST (IRE) 62 S1 — b g Presenting-Snipe Hunt — W P Mullins (IRE) Mrs S Ricci	8 ¹Jonathan Burke	10-8 (168)
33	/2957-F	LORD WINDERMERE (IRE) 126 S4 — b g Oscar-Satellite Dancer — J H Culloty (IRE) Dr R Lambe	12 ¹A E Lynch	10-7 (166)
34	2-36121	CAPTAIN REDBEARD (IRE) 84 (35H) S3 — ch g Bach-Diesel Dancer — Stuart Coltherd S Coltherd	9 Sam Coltherd	10-7 (168)
35	-1663P3	HOUBLON DES OBEAUX (FR) 20 S3 — b g Panoramic-Harkosa — Venetia Williams Exors Of The Late Mrs J Blackwell	b 11 Charlie Deutsch	10-7 (170)
36	6-PP1FP	BLESS THE WINGS (IRE) 12 S1 — b g Winged Love-Silva Venture — Gordon Elliott (IRE) Adrian Butler/S P O'Connor	p 13 Jack Kennedy	10-6 (175)
37	-63U152	MILANSBAR (IRE) 28 S5 — b g Milan-Ardenhar — Neil King Robert Bothway	b 11 Bryony Frost	10-6 (174)
38	F6-2359	FINAL NUDGE (IRE) 30 S7 — b g Kayf Tara-Another Shot — David Dennis Corbett Stud & Andrew George	p 9 Gavin Sheehan	10-6 (171)
39	3-4UP84	DOUBLE ROSS (IRE) 30 S3 — ch g Double Eclipse-Kinross — Nigel Twiston-Davies Options O Syndicate	12 Tom Bellamy	10-6 (170)
40	85-090P	ROAD TO RICHES (IRE) 30 S3 — b g Gamut-Bellora — Noel Meade (IRE) Gigginstown House Stud	t11 Sean Flanagan	10-5 (170)

2017 (40 ran) One For Arthur Lucinda Russell 8 10-11 14/1 Derek Fox OR148

POSTDATA	Tiger Roll	RP RATING	Anibale Fly

▶▶FORM: PAGE 92, STATS: NEXT PAGE

▶▶THUNDER AND ROSES, who carries 10-5, is number 1 on the card because it was brought into the race as first reserve following the withdrawal of Minella Rocco, the original number 1.
▶▶DELUSIONOFGRANDEUR, who carries 10-5, is number 12 on the card because it was brought into the race as second reserve following the withdrawal of Vincente, the original number 12.
▶▶WALK IN THE MILL, who carries 10-4, is number 24 on the card because it was brought into the race as second reserve following the withdrawal of Beeves, the original number 24.

BETTING FORECAST: 10 Anibale Fly, Total Recall, 11 Blaklion, Tiger Roll, 14 Seeyouatmidnight, 16 Baie Des Iles, The Last Samuri, 20 I Just Know, Ucello Conti, 25 Captain Redbeard, Pleasant Company, Raz de Maree, Regal Encore, The Dutchman, 33 Alpha Des Obeaux, Gas Line Boy, Milansbar, Shantou Flyer, Vieux Lion Rouge, 40 Houblon Des Obeaux, 50 Bless The Wings, Buywise, Carlingford Lough, Chase The Spud, Final Nudge, Saint Are, Valseur Lido, Warriors Tale, 66 Childrens List, Double Ross, Lord Windermere, Pendra, Perfect Candidate, Road To Riches, Virgilio, 100 Maggio, Tenor Nivernais.

SPOTLIGHT RICHARD AUSTEN'S VERDICT

With yesterday's rain, the ground may well have swung sufficiently in favour of the veteran **RAZ DE MAREE (nap)**, who can now follow up January's win on heavy going in the Welsh National. He's not the best of jumpers, but a slower pace on deep ground will be a help to him in that respect and it will greatly boost his chances of reeling in the leaders. On the other hand, the going might just have gone against the otherwise appealing each-way option **Bless The Wings** and leaves those who make big steps up in distance with more to prove. While **Blaklion** and **The Last Samuri** have excelled here, they need to do better off today's marks, so the second choice is **I Just Know**, who impressed with his staying power over 3m6f on soft going at Catterick. **Baie Des Iles** could also prove well suited by today's test, while **Warriors Tale**, **Maggio** and **Anibale Fly** appeal most among those untested over a marathon trip.

LORD SEFTON STAND
RANDOX HEALTH
RANDOX HEALTH
HEALTH
RANDOX HEALTH GRAND NAT

'He'll love the trip and the nice ground if it dries out at Aintree,' he said. 'I think he definitely has a serious chance, but it's just a pity he doesn't have enough weight for me to ride him.'

On being asked how it felt to win on Tiger Roll at the Cheltenham Festival, he added: 'It felt unreal and better than I could have expected it to – I really felt on top of the world.

'That moment meant so much to me and I was quite emotional as I crossed the line. After missing Labaik winning the Supreme Novices' Hurdle last year I didn't want to see anyone or even leave the house. This year wherever I go people are congratulating me and saying "well done", so it's been brilliant.'

The rider's confidence was matched by Michael O'Leary, who also planned to run Alpha Des Obeaux, Road To Riches and Valseur Lido alongside his three-time festival hero.

O'Leary said: 'If he can survive as far as Becher's Brook the first time round it would be great. I'd say there'd be gaps in the fences after that.'

Elliott first launched a world-record assault on the BoyleSports Irish Grand National at Fairyhouse on Easter Monday and it paid off when General Principle pulled off a last-gasp victory, giving his trainer a much-desired first triumph in the race.

Punters latched on to Tiger Roll as the positive noises continued from connections.

Elliott believed that Tiger Roll, who would be ridden by Davy Russell for the first time since the Punchestown festival in May 2014, would rise to the Aintree challenge.

'I think he'll love the National,' Elliott said. 'The fences will light him up. It's the Grand National, and you need a lot of luck and for everything to go right, but I think the race will suit him.'

Tiger Roll didn't disappoint, as Jon Lees reported:

It may be the nation's biggest race, but at Aintree yesterday size did not matter as the pint-sized Tiger Roll showed gallons of courage to claim the Randox Health Grand National – but it was mighty close.

In a climax fought out between Ireland's two dominant jumps stables, the Gordon Elliott-trained Tiger Roll had coasted to the front at the second-last fence, striding clear of a seemingly beaten Pleasant Company from the Willie Mullins camp and who had made a lot of the running.

Yet, as the noise from the stands reached crescendo pitch to acclaim Davy Russell and Tiger Roll up the run-in, their six-length lead began to evaporate. David Mullins and Pleasant Company were not done after all.

Rattling home, the pair finished right upsides Tiger Roll at the post in a finish so close that neither jockey was confident who had won before the photo-finish delivered the verdict to 10-1 Tiger Roll by a head, delivering second Grand National triumphs for Elliott and owner Michael O'Leary, and a first for Russell.

In 13 previous rides in the race Russell, 38, the oldest jockey in the National and soon to be crowned champion of Ireland, came closest to winning last year when third on Saint Are.

But Russell's first thoughts in his big moment were for others as he dedicated his win to Flat jockey Pat Smullen, who has been diagnosed with a tumour.

He added: 'I'm thinking about my kids at home knowing they can be part of this wonderful event. I've been coming for years and been satisfied leaving not winning, because it's such a marvellous event. It's just amazing to have finally done it. Now to have won it, I don't know what to say.'

Tiger Roll and Davy Russell clear the water jump in the Grand National

Previous spread: Davy Russell sits back (right) as Tiger Roll heads over the Canal Turn

This page: Tiger Roll is over the final fence with just the run-in to negotiate

Russell lost his mother Phyllis before the Cheltenham Festival and added: 'Mam passed recently and she was a marvellous woman. She got me out of bed at 6am to drive me around the country.

'She always knew it was worthwhile for her child. I've had a brilliant career and I hope everyone who has helped me along the way can enjoy this as much as I will.'

Tiger Roll already had a remarkable career record, having won three times at the Cheltenham Festival, the latest in the Cross Country Chase.

Russell had been worried the eight-year-old, who at 15.2hh was described by his owner Michael O'Leary as 'a little rat of a thing', would not take to the National fences because by racehorse standards he was small, but there was never any cause for alarm.

Of the major pre-race fancies, Blaklion was brought down at the first, I Just Know came down at Becher's Brook, which had to be bypassed on the second circuit as Charlie Deutsch was being treated after falling from Houblon Des Obeaux, and 7-1 favourite Total Recall pulled up after making a sequence of blunders.

By the time Pleasant Company led a breakaway quintet towards the second-last fence, it was Tiger Roll travelling conspicuously the best.

He helped secure a clean sweep of the first four placings for Ireland as Bless The Wings, also trained by Elliott, hung on for third by a neck from Anibale Fly in fourth, while Milansbar gave Bryony Frost a brilliant Grand National debut to complete in fifth.

Defeat was agony for Mullins, who at least could console himself that he had tasted victory in the race two years ago on Rule The World.

As the finish unfolded O'Leary, who also owned Rule The World, said: 'We were all celebrating, but at the line we were all panicking. Some people don't think I have a heart but I can tell you it was beating very hard and very fast for the last 100 yards of that race.'

The Ryanair boss, who once sacked Russell as his retained jockey, added: 'It's a wonderful day for Davy; everyone knows we've had our ups and downs but he's always come back better and stronger. It's fitting that he's coming to the end of his career and he now has a Grand National on his CV.'

Elliott's 2007 National win with Silver Birch was to mark the start of what has become a phenomenal training career.

He said: 'I probably didn't appreciate it that much the first time as I was younger, but now I'm a bit wiser. Tiger Roll is unbelievable.

'I'm going home on the boat tonight. Michael probably doesn't want to hear that but Ryanair flights are too dear. The horse will be paraded tomorrow and there will be a lot of drinking.'

RACING POST ANALYSIS – Mark Brown

There were 38 runners at the start and just 12 managed to finish, with plenty of casualties on the first circuit. The first four home were all Irish-trained and two pulled 11 lengths clear, with the remarkable Tiger Roll just clinging on from the rallying Pleasant Company. The ground took its toll on some of the runners and Becher's had to be bypassed second time around due to a stricken jockey. A step up from both Tiger Roll and Pleasant Company, the former just a couple of pounds shy of the average level of the winner for the past ten years.

Tiger Roll is an incredible horse and coasted his way through this, the toughest of races, overcoming both ground and jumping fears and clinging on to record a famous victory. A son of Derby winner Authorized, and winner of the Triumph Hurdle back in 2014, he's added other notable wins in the National Hunt Chase and Cross Country at Cheltenham over the past 13 months and really took to the race naturally, being well placed throughout under the masterful Davy Russell and bounding into a clear lead after the last. He began to empty close to home, though, possibly getting a little lonely also, but the line came just in time, as in another stride he was second. Just an eight-year-old, all roads for this hardy performer will presumably lead back here next season.

AINTREE
April 14, 2018
Randox Health Grand National Handicap Chase
4m2½f

1 Tiger Roll	Davy Russell	10-1
2 Pleasant Company	David Mullins	25-1
3 Bless The Wings	Jack Kennedy	40-1

head, 11 lengths
38 ran

Tiger Roll is all out to win by a head from
Pleasant Company

Later, Russell spoke more about Pat Smullen and what winning the Grand National meant to him:

When the first microphone was thrust in his face at this crowning moment of his career, Davy Russell took himself out of the story. 'This one is for Pat Smullen. I was speaking to him the other morning, and he's as tough as nails, so this one is for Pat,' he said.

Only a couple of weeks before, Smullen, the nine-time Irish champion Flat jockey, had revealed his cancer diagnosis. The news left the close-knit world of Irish racing in shock.

As Russell spoke you knew this was his way of putting things in perspective. It was done with directness and dignity. His first thoughts were for a fellow jockey facing a challenge from within his own body. Then, having had a minute or so to let the experience of the past nine minutes and forty seconds sink in, he allowed himself a moment of self-reflection.

'I have won this race a thousand times in my head, in my dreams, as a child,' he said. Russell recalled childhood days, building miniature Aintree-style fences with cut grass in the garden of his County Cork home.

For a hard man in an unforgiving profession he can be surprisingly lyrical at times.

Russell has travelled a long road, not always a smooth one. He has seldom been short on self-belief. There was a sense that perhaps he always felt this was his destiny.

Davy Russell punches the air in celebration after claiming his first victory in the Grand National

Tom Kerr was also on hand to witness a remarkable triumph:

The look of relief on Davy Russell's face as the judge announced the decision amid the deafening silence of 70,000 expectant spectators said it all – Aintree had almost just seen a story of defeat being snatched from the jaws of victory to rank alongside Devon Loch's infamous belly-flop.

It had all looked so straightforward passing the Elbow, as Tiger Roll, this tiny horse with a giant heart, strode clear of Pleasant Company looking for all the world like he could go round this marathon course a second time.

It still looked straightforward with a half a furlong to go, Tiger Roll seemingly set to coast home in isolation, a National winner feted in triumphal fashion.

Roman generals of old would be reminded by a whispering slave they were mortal lest the adulation of the citizenry give them notions of diefication.

At Aintree that reminder was not whispered but screamed by the charging Pleasant Company, who with the post little more than a heartbeat away discovered a second wind – or was it a third or fourth? – and came flying to the horror and amazement of the heaving grandstands.

The margin determined by the judge after a wait of moments that seemed to stretch to hours was a head. There have been closer National finishes – not many – but few as dramatic as this.

For all that Pleasant Company ran a magnificent race under a genius ride by David Mullins, defeat would have been the toughest of conclusions for Tiger Roll and Davy Russell, a partnership that might have been made in racing heaven.

Tiger Roll, for one, is nothing short of a superstar of the sport who only the stoniest heart could fail to be moved by.

He is a mere slip of an animal, but he would run through a wall for you then stop to give it a boot for good measure.

He has won three times at the Cheltenham Festival – over hurdles at two miles, over fences at four miles and over every obstacle chaos can devise in the madcap Cross Country just last month.

Now he has conquered the mighty National fences, a David to their Goliath.

At Cheltenham, Ryanair boss Michael O'Leary, who owns Tiger Roll as part of the Gigginstown House Stud operation, described the horse with a sort of brutal poetry as 'a little rat of a thing, but he's got a heart of a lion'. Some heart, some horse.

Russell is a legend of the sport but like so many weighing room greats before him the National had eluded him throughout the prime of his career. At 38, he was the oldest jockey in the race. He put all that experience to good use.

Russell was brilliant on his most willing partner, even unfazed at losing an iron early in the second circuit, and he gave Tiger Roll backers not another moment's panic – at least until that last-gasp

Gordon Elliott runs over to congratulate Davy Russell and Tiger Roll

fright – with an impeccably judged round of jumping around the sport's most challenging fences.

It was a mark of the man that in the wild emotion of the aftermath celebrations and relief were joined by a dedication to fellow jockey Pat Smullen, currently fighting a brain tumour. 'He's tough as nails,' he said.

Russell was fired as Gigginstown's retained jockey in 2014, infamously after being asked to join O'Leary for a 'cup of tea', but has continued to ride for them and especially for trainer Gordon Elliott, whose all-conquering exploits reached a fresh plane with this victory.

It was 2007 when Elliott won his first Grand National with Silver Birch. He was just 29 then and taking his first steps as a trainer – he had not even won a single race in Ireland, an achievement which would not follow for several weeks after his Aintree victory.

How things have changed – now Elliott bestrides the world of jump racing as a genuine colossus.

He has been Cheltenham Festival top trainer for the past two seasons, is odds-on to dethrone Willie Mullins and land a first Irish trainers' championship, and has now achieved a feat few trainers ever manage in winning a second Grand National.

Elliott is just 40. You wouldn't bet against him picking up a third – or a fourth.

The bookmakers were left licking their wounds, as Bruce Jackson reported:

Punters put a Tiger in their tank to leave bookmakers counting the cost of another Gordon Elliott-trained Grand National winner which sparked what layers called 'a multi-million pound payout'.

Total Recall may have gone off 7-1 market leader but Tiger Roll, the 10-1 winner, had been one of the best-backed horses with many bookmakers in the run-up to the race and began the day as one of the 12-1 co-favourites.

Coral were cheering on 25-1 chance Pleasant Company as he closed relentlessly near the line, with spokesman David Stevens saying: 'Tiger Roll was one of the most popular selections throughout the busiest and biggest betting day of the year, and his many backers were counting their money when he jumped the last.

Gordon Elliott with the trophy after winning the Grand National for the second time

Davy Russell is congratulated as he leaves the course on Tiger Roll

Previous spread: Tiger Roll has a clear lead over Pleasant Company as he reaches the Elbow

'We were given hope when Pleasant Company fought back, but it wasn't to be. In one of the closest National finishes ever it was the punters who came out on top, sparking a multi-million pound payout.'

Ladbrokes' spokeswoman Nicola McGeady said: 'It is a result that has left the betting industry licking their wounds with a multi-million pound payout.'

Paul Binfield, for Paddy Power, said: 'We've literally been rolled over – that was the worst result in the book by a long way.'

Lawrence Lyons, spokesman for fellow Irish firm BoyleSports, said: 'It was one of the most open Grand Nationals in recent history but with Irish horses filling the first four places and another in sixth it was one of our worst results in recent memory.

'Tiger Roll was by far the biggest loser in our book and with the poor places we had no respite.'

Betfred boss Fred Done said: 'Punters roared home the well-fancied Tiger Roll and Davy Russell earned his stripes. It was a costly National.'

Tiger Roll was the worst result for Betway, with spokesman Alan Alger reporting: 'He's cost us an absolute fortune. We laid a number of big bets just before the off, including one punter who had £4,000 each-way at 12-1 – he was well and truly the worst possible result.'

Bet365 reported record turnover on the race and a losing book, and the firm's Pat Cooney said: 'Tiger Roll was our biggest liability on the off, but the places were okay. It was a losing race for us.'

Michael Shinners, of Sky Bet, added: 'Tiger Roll was popular after his Cheltenham exploits and after some bookmaker-friendly Grand Nationals this was certainly one for the backers.'

Alastair Down offered further reflections on Tiger Roll's victory:

You can, if you will excuse the expression, stuff your overnight sensations and one-hit wonders up your jumper.

True legends grow in the telling and Tiger Roll, whom you could slot through a tube of Polo mints without touching the sides, cleaved himself even closer to jump racing's throbbing heart with a Grand National triumph that flirted with coronary country to emerge rampantly celebratory.

Coming to the Elbow the engravers were already chiselling the hugely popular Tiger Roll's name on the trophy. But in the last 100 yards he began to empty like a basin of water and, with the winning line no more than an arm's length away, it looked as though success was about to gurgle down the plughole as David Mullins drew a phenomenal late rattle from Pleasant Company.

But this is Tiger Roll we are talking about, a little bouncing ball of indomitability, and the worldly-wise wily Davy Russell held on by a fast-evaporating head.

A tiger indeed, and what a weapon of war he has been. With his customary silver tongue Michael O'Leary described the winner as a 'little rat of a thing' but, as in the famous book, he is King Rat.

If you must have an animal analogy then settle for rabbit – as in Flanagan and Allen's 'Run rabbit, run rabbit, run run run', because that is Tiger Roll's forte and he'll run for you unflinching until hell has long frozen over.

He has won three different races at the festival and now a Grand National. That is indeed the road less travelled, and only two horses – both among chasing's all time greats – have ever trod an even vaguely similar one.

Golden Miller stands supreme with five Gold Cups and a National, while L'Escargot netted the old Gloucester Hurdle and a brace of Gold Cups before going on to beat Red Rum at Aintree in 1975.

Tiger Roll is not on a par with that pair. They are lofty titans, whereas this tough diamond is more the horse next door.

He cost £80,000 and has now won £802,000. At just 15.2, that is an awful lot of grand per hand.

But, at the risk of raining on the winner's parade, don't fall for all this guff about what 'an unbelievable job Gordon Elliott has done with this horse'. It is pure nonsense, as any village's idiot could train Tiger Roll.

We all know certain horses 'come to themselves' at a particular time of year. Well, this pocket Hercules keeps it much simpler than that.

He won his Triumph Hurdle on March 14, his National Hunt Chase on March 14 and the Cross Country on March 14. Now he has won the Grand National on April 14.

You don't need a training manual with this horse – all that's required is a diary. Time of the year indeed – Tiger Roll has it down to day of the month. The steeplechaser as Swiss watch.

He will have a break now and we'll next see him in the July Cup on July 14. The National was a triumph shot through with heart-warming subplots and we will start with the up close and personal part, where the real work is done.

Tiger Roll's groom Louise Dunne is the mother of two sets of twins. So she has to wash and clean up after Tiger Roll and a couple of others then go home and do the same for four offspring from two foalings.

She is a permanent fixture leading up yearlings and jumpers at the sales and at Punchestown last year rode in a charity race for stable staff who had never ridden a winner. She won that of course and, with a 100 per cent record, promptly retired from race-riding – people are just born lazy and she clearly spends most of the day with her feet up.

After producing one set of twins she went in to be scanned during the second battle of the bulge and when told two more were on the way her entirely understandable response was: 'You've got to be fecking joking!' As Pleasant Company came to scythe down her pride and joy in the last ten yards on Saturday she must have been

Davy Russell holds aloft the Grand National trophy after fulfilling a childhood dream at Aintree

having kittens to add to the twins. God knows when she sleeps, but after cleaning her house it must be a case – in more ways than one – of Dunne and dusted.

And, of course, this was a defining moment for Davy Russell, who can look a bit dour but is both warm and genuinely witty – qualities that have made him a cult figure at Ireland's 930 Cheltenham Festival previews, where he brings the house down more often than a demolition man.

Back in 2013 he was sacked by Michael O'Leary over an instantly notorious cup of tea. 'Sorry Davy,' O'Leary said, 'we're out of sugar – one lump of cyanide or two?' Of course it was a hammer blow, but pride and resilience saw him through and drove him to fresh heights.

His humanity shone through after the race and encompassed a wonderful tale of childhood and fresh-cut grass. He said: 'No motor mowers in those days, but I used to love raking up the grass and

A proud Gordon Elliott with Tiger Roll the day after his Grand National victory

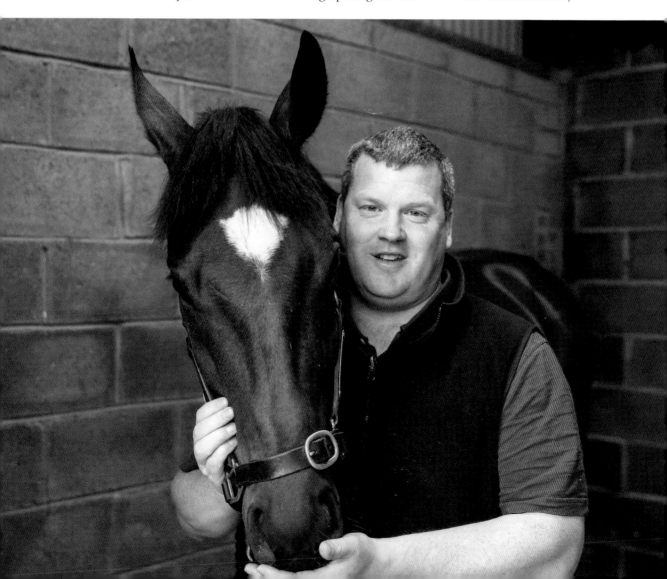

making imaginary Aintree fences and kicking through the top of them, just like they do here. I've won thousands of Nationals!' You would think Russell had just been out for a hack across the fields. But Tiger Roll brushed through the top of several fences and his rider momentarily lost an iron at the 19th.

But by God, Davy got some tune out of the winner, whom he last sat on four years ago. Some horses travel through a race, but Tiger Roll just bombed through it to the manner born.

And, let's face it, Triumph Hurdle winners are not the stuff of Aintree. The only comparable horse of recent times was Commanche Court, who beat 27 others when winning the 1997 Triumph before they gelded the race, landed the 2000 Irish National and was beaten only one and three-quarter lengths by Best Mate in the 2002 Gold Cup and might have won if he hadn't tried to bring the second-last home with him.

But if God loves a trier then so do the racing public and they have taken the little horse to their hearts. He seems to have been around since the days of the dodo but takes everything thrown at him and is at his most lethal when getting up from the canvas as you know he will come back punching.

I thought David Mullins was brilliant on the runner-up, who was going every bit as well as Tiger Roll three out but just landed skew-whiff two out and began to struggle. But Mullins sat and went for it only from the last before reaching for the kitchen sink coming to the Elbow.

He drew a screeching surge from Pleasant Company, who was ahead a stride past the line. But at least he has a National in the bag already via Rule The World.

And what do you say about the O'Leary brothers, Michael and Eddie? One lord of the skies, the other lord of the sales.

Eddie is a genius and, like many of them, a touch mad. He and Mags O'Toole make for a lethal pair of judges. Some buyers and agents appear in the winner's enclosure like moths round a lamp when one they have bought goes in.

You never see O'Toole seeking that limelight, but Michael was having none of that on Saturday and forced Mags on to the podium and paid eloquent tribute to her at his press conference.

Some years ago, after a very lean Cheltenham, Michael O'Leary said: 'What we need is faster slow horses.' Last month Gigginstown had seven festival winners – mission accomplished.

You felt for the extraordinary Willie Mullins but we have Gordon Elliott to thank for preventing a Mullinsopoly that was what the sport once threatened to become. Willie knows competition is great and had a smile on his face when saying 'though I could do without it!' But jump racing is the beneficiary.

The final footnote to the day came late in the evening on a Ryanair flight. Michael O'Leary's voice came over the air personally apologising for the ten-minute delay and saying: 'Unusually on this flight there will be a free bar – one drink each!' And so it was that a small horse bought the happy passengers a large one.

David Jennings went to Tiger Roll's homecoming in County Meath the day after the National:

So this is what a Grand National winner looks like. Short, slim and, some might even say, scrawny. There ain't much of him.

Grand National winners are not supposed to look like this. Tiger Roll would never get a modelling gig; pep talks to soldiers the week before a war would be more his thing.

The streets of Summerhill in County Meath have staged something like this before. A little more than two years ago a beautiful brute of an animal paraded up and down the town with hundreds of eyes glued to his gorgeousness. That was 2016 Cheltenham Gold Cup winner Don Cossack. This is Tiger Roll – more gutsy than glamorous, more Roy Keane than Ronaldo.

It has just ticked past 2.35pm on a soggy Sunday when Tiger Roll starts to strut down the street with groom Louise Dunne, who has not stopped smiling since she stopped crying shortly after the photo-finish verdict was called. Following him is Irish Grand National winner General Principle and Bless The Wings, 11 lengths back in third on Saturday. They must feel like Colin Farrell's mates on a night out. Nobody even notices them.

Tiger Roll looked like he could not move another yard when he stopped to a crawl in the final 100 yards on Saturday, but he's been a busy boy since. A second lap of the village is swiftly followed by a plethora of pictures. He does not bat an eyelid. Maybe he doesn't have the energy.

'He's just amazing,' says Dunne. 'Everyone goes on about his size, but his size doesn't matter. All that matters is his heart. He's grumpy but very lovable. He's some character. He'd have no problem letting you know if he didn't want you in the stable. He's a quirky fella and you need to know him.'

This commotion is all new to Tiger Roll, but not to his trainer. He knows the drill. There are selfies to smile for, hundreds of hands

Following spread: Tiger Roll is led through the streets of Summerhill by Karen Morgan (left) and Louise Dunne

79

Top: A homemade sign welcomes Tiger Roll back to Summerhill

Middle: Well-wishers line the streets

Bottom: Anita O'Leary and Gordon Elliott hold the trophy with Tiger Roll

to shake and people to pretend to know. Elliott's home is less than a mile down the road so failure to recognise a face might never be forgiven, no matter how long ago he saw it.

'It's unbelievable,' he says while shaking his head. 'I think it's only starting to sink in now. To be home here in Summerhill and see so many familiar faces, so many friends and family, is something else. There's a great buzz around the place and I'm sure it will be a long night!' That you can guarantee. Parties have a habit of lasting longer than they should around here. They stay longer than Tiger Roll himself. The pints are already being poured in Swan's pub and it won't be long before Elliott gets his first sip.

He didn't drink a drop the night before; he knew what lay ahead. He knew only too well he would have to reflect on the race hundreds of times.

Hangovers don't work at occasions like this.

Time for another recollection, Gordon. 'About 200 yards out I thought he was home and hosed,' he begins. 'I was sure he was going to hack up. He's only small, though, so four miles and two and a half furlongs was going to be tough on him. In the last 100 yards he hit a brick wall, but thank God the line came in time.

'He's been a super little horse. To win at three Cheltenham Festivals and a Grand National is amazing. I'm very proud of him.'

Despite soaring into the air and clenching his fist tightly as the photo-finish result was finally called, surely Elliott knew Tiger Roll had held on? He replies: 'I didn't know, I genuinely didn't. I wasn't sure of the angle at Aintree. I could tell you the angles at the winning line of every track in Ireland, but I'm not too familiar with the ones in England. I was very nervous before the result was called. It was pure relief when it was.'

So what's this Tiger Roll like then? 'He's actually a little bit like a tiger,' comes the reply. 'He can be in great form one day, terrible form the next. He's either very good or very bad, that's just the way he is.

'In fairness, he's allowed to be in bad form whenever he wants because, when he's good, he's very good.'

Ollie Smith, from a few miles down the road in Robinstown, was one of the many punters glad he was very good on Saturday. He backed him, but a friend of his fiancée got a much better price than he did.

That fiancée, Sarah Parsons, says: 'A friend of mine backed him at 50-1 when the weights came out a few months ago. She only had a euro each-way but certainly got the value.'

Elliott was top trainer at Cheltenham last month and has now won the Grand National again, 11 years after Silver Birch. Is the final chapter of a fairy-tale campaign going to be penned at Punchestown? 'Whatever happens we've had a great season, but if we do win the trainers' title there will be an even bigger party to the one you see here today,' says Elliott, daring to dream.

A first championship can wait. For now let's just appreciate the tenacious, terrific Tiger Roll.

Russell had no time for celebrating, though, as he went to Tramore the day after the National as Brian Sheerin reported:

Davy Russell would have been forgiven for joining in on the Grand National celebrations taking place near Gordon Elliott's Longwood-based yard in County Meath rather than making the trip south to Tramore, but the Aintree hero stayed true to his word, much to the delight of local trainer John Kiely.

Less than 24 hours after guiding Tiger Roll to a memorable Grand National success, Russell picked up from where he had left off aboard the Kiely-trained Decision Time in the opening maiden hurdle. The trainer admitted he would have forgiven the 38-year-old had he not fulfilled the engagement.

Davy Russell with his family at Punchestown in April 2018

Kiely said: 'I doubted whether or not he'd be here after yesterday I must say, as he was being dragged here, there and everywhere, but I'm delighted he came.

'It's brilliant. What a thrill to give him his first winner after his big day yesterday. He gave Tiger Roll a great ride.'

For Russell, there was never any doubt about him coming here; the soon-to-be-crowned champion jockey revealed he'd made a promise to his kids he couldn't break.

After securing a quick double on Elliott-trained Monatomic in the following maiden hurdle, he said: 'I went straight home last night.

'I'd promised the kids I'd be home and I was happier going home to be honest anyway as coming here half-cocked would have been no good to anyone – plus, Lily [Russell's daughter] would have killed me!'

Reflecting on Tiger Roll and the emotion and adulation the victory stirred up among his family, friends and fans, he added: 'The Grand National takes in everybody. I've met an awful lot of people through my career and I hope they can enjoy it as much as I did.'

Russell's father Jerry, who had his colours carried to victory last summer when Youghal By The Sea won a bumper at Bellewstown, was not at Aintree to see his son but was present at Tramore.

'In England you have to turn off your phones when you're on course, but I rang dad straight away after we left the course and it was great,' said Russell.

'I intend on catching up on the celebrations with Gordon and everyone tonight, and we can give it a good whack later!'

There were further thoughts from Lee Mottershead on what the victory meant for the race:

What shone through so vividly in the latest unforgettable chapter of the Grand National is how much it still means to all those who yearn to win it.

The old race has been changed considerably. The fences are a bit smaller and the distance a little shorter but the race's standing is every bit as tall and mighty as ever. You had only to see the reactions of Davy Russell, Gordon Elliott, Michael O'Leary – and, indeed, David Mullins – for proof.

It was perhaps most evident in the face and words of Russell. Here is a man well into the back nine of his career. He has added his name to so many of the sport's crown jewels, not least the

Cheltenham Gold Cup, yet he made it absolutely clear this topped everything that had gone before.

The Grand National touches us in a way no other horserace comes close to managing. We love it, we care about it and we have worried for it. Listening to Russell talking about building pretend Aintree fences after his father mowed the lawn was moving and endearing.

'I've won this race a thousand times in my head, in my dreams as a child,' he said. You could tell he meant it. You could see this moment was his personal crowning glory.

It is a moment Elliott and O'Leary had experienced before. Experiencing it again was no less enjoyable, with the Ryanair magnate so overwhelmed he told fellow passengers on his flight back to Dublin there would be a free bar, for which he would personally pay – albeit with no more than one free.

In Tiger Roll – so shrewdly snapped up for Gigginstown by agent Mags O'Toole after winning at Market Rasen – O'Leary owns a simply astonishing little horse. Thanks to him, all future Triumph Hurdle winners who end up contesting Champion Hurdles will seem boring and unadventurous.

The tiny Tiger is a warrior, just like Pleasant Company. Saturday's marvellous runner-up raced with a zest that was a joy to behold before rallying so gamely under Mullins, whose face briefly turned into a picture of pain when the photo-finish verdict was announced. Thereafter, the hero of 2016 – who was then in Gigginstown silks – spoke and acted with the sort of sportsmanship one expects of jump jockeys.

Similarly magnanimous in defeat was Pleasant Company's trainer Willie Mullins.

A few days before the race I suggested one potential storyline for the National involving the rivalry of Mullins and Elliott. That said, nobody could have expected the two trainers who dominated the Cheltenham Festival to totally dominate the most watched of all finishes in such gripping manner.

What happened in those heart-stopping closing stages told the story the season will finish with. For just as Pleasant Company was frustrated in his furious pursuit of Tiger Roll, so, too, has Mullins found reeling in Elliott hitherto impossible, in Cheltenham's league table and the fight for the Irish trainers' championship.

Such has been their burning desire to be crowned champion they kept the majority of their stars away from Aintree, mindful that Punchestown and its handsome prize money will decide their tussle. Even so, they were responsible for the first three home in a Grand National that concluded with seven of the ten horses who earned prize money representing Ireland.

We creep closer to what will be a thoroughly absorbing Punchestown festival, during which Mullins last year somehow managed a prize money swing of around €600,000. That proved to be more than enough. If he can replicate such a swing it will again be enough, but only just.

At the moment, Mullins faces a mission that is not impossible but improbable. Year in, year out, the Grand National serves up similarly improbable but wonderfully memorable stories.

Thanks to Tiger Roll and his team, the latest story was one of the best.

Martin Stevens spoke to Jerry O'Brien for his thoughts on what Tiger Roll had now achieved:

It might not have been Jerry O'Brien's intention to breed a Grand National winner when he sent his mare Swiss Roll to Authorized in 2009 – 'I thought the resultant foal would win a few Gold Cups,' he says wryly – but he is nevertheless bursting with pride at having produced this year's Aintree hero, the tenacious Tiger Roll.

After dabbling in several different careers, including a stint grave-digging, O'Brien was a long-time member of the Coolmore veterinary team until he retired to his farm near Portroe in County Tipperary in the noughties.

Tiger Roll's dam Swiss Roll (left) winning at Galway in July 2004

Tiger Roll's sire Authorized wins the Juddmonte
International at York in August 2007

'I worked for Stan Cosgrove on the Curragh and anything
I profess to know about veterinary is due to Stan,' he says.
'Subsequently I left for France on a grape-picking expedition and
then worked in New Zealand and South Africa, as the rugby ethos
in both countries fascinated me. Next it was on to Trinity College,
where I studied History of Art for a year.'

History of Art might sound a strange diversion for a former
veterinary student, but as O'Brien explains: 'For better or worse I
practised the art of veterinary medicine rather than the science as I
found the science bewildering.

'The technology nowadays is fantastic, but over-reliance on it can
sometimes cloud one's innate common-sense judgement.'

The instinctive approach must have served O'Brien well at
Coolmore as he enjoyed a long spell there, from the stud's inception
in the 1970s until 2005.

'I joined "Coolmore Cares" initially for one year,' he says.
'Twenty-seven years later after some wondrous times it was a case
of, as the bookies say, when the fun stops, stop. In college terms, I
dropped out. Non, je ne regrette rien.

'My brief at Coolmore was reproduction. It's not rocket science.
If you moved with nature, most would get pregnant in spite of
you.

'It gets a bit tricky if you have 15 for the one sire and you can
only cover three or four but, like kicking penalties, if you do it often
enough one gets proficient and after working for four or five seasons
for Stan Cosgrove you could do it in your sleep.'

O'Brien has given up the veterinary work since leaving Coolmore because 'practising after Coolmore would be a total anti-climax: it would be like going from a five-star hotel to a B&B,' he says.

'With the facilities we had we were able to dot the i's and cross the t's. I had a great team of people at various stages in the car with me – Bill Magner, Michael Andree, Bill Dwan, Tom Lynch, Brian O'Neill, Padraig Dolan, Eric Ward and my great mate Christy Grassick, who gave us free rein. They were blokes you could scrum down with every day. I couldn't have performed or survived without them.'

O'Brien was bitten by the breeding bug while at Coolmore and among the broodmares he bought was one who would give him most of his success, and is indeed the granddam of Tiger Roll. That was On Air, a daughter of Chief Singer who was a useful middle-distance handicapper on the Flat and also won a Haydock novice hurdle and finished fourth to Berude Not To in the Grade 2 Kennel Gate Castle Novices' Hurdle.

On Air produced four winners for O'Brien, including Berenson, a son of Entrepreneur who took a Curragh maiden and finished second to Dubawi in the National Stakes on his only two starts; Pollen, an Orpen mare who carried the breeder's silks to victory in the Park Express Stakes; and Khachaturian, a Spectrum gelding who won on the Flat, over hurdles and over fences.

Tiger Roll's dam – Swiss Roll, a sister to Berenson – completed the quartet of winners for On Air. She scored in two races and claimed second in the Vintage Crop Stakes before she joined her dam on O'Brien's stud.

The daughter has matched the mother's feat of producing four winners, headed by the Lonsdale Cup winner and Irish St Leger runner-up Ahzeemah (to Dubawi) as well as Tiger Roll (to Authorized).

Her three-year-old colt, Austrian School, is held in high regard by trainer Mark Johnston with the son of Teofilo, bought by the trainer as a yearling for just 20,000gns, having won two of his four starts in 2017.

The mare has a two-year-old filly and yearling colt, both also by Teofilo, and she is in foal to Exceed And Excel.

Authorized and Teofilo are by sons of Sadler's Wells in Montjeu and Galileo, while Entrepreneur was also by Sadler's Wells, so Tiger Roll and Austrian School are inbred 3x3 to the late Coolmore great.

O'Brien explains the rationale behind the matings that led to Tiger Roll's birth.

He says: 'On Air came in season so I asked Tom Lynch at Coolmore who he considered to be the best-looking stallion on the

Tommy Stack trained Tiger Roll's dam Swiss Roll

stud at the time. He replied Entrepreneur, so I said, "Put the blue tag on her, Tom."

'Swiss Roll arrived as the result and she was sent to Tommy Stack, who did a marvellous job training her to win and get black type. She was a nightmare – a bad traveller who worried a lot and ate very little. But she gave everything.

'Tiger Roll would not have come into existence but for being a foal share that the late Michael Buckley at Kildangan Stud generously offered to me in Authorized.

'He was a little concerned about the close inbreeding to Sadler's Wells but I said, "Mick, let's take the mystery out of it," as I thought you can't have enough Sadler's Wells in a pedigree.'

And what was the Grand National and triple Cheltenham Festival hero like when he was merely a tiger cub? 'He was a most correct foal, with a wonderfully intelligent head,' O'Brien says. 'He would willingly do anything for you, but I learned at an early stage that if I took him on I'd lose that battle.'

Tiger Roll was a beneficiary of the same natural approach to husbandry that O'Brien implemented during his veterinary career.

'I try to wean as late as possible, a month before the mares foal or a month before they go to the sale – basically endeavouring as much as possible to replicate nature,' he says. 'In fact, Berenson was weaned as a yearling as On Air was running late.

'I keep it simple. The foals receive no supplements, no vitamin injections and so on. Tiger and his mum were fed on the cooked mix.

Tiger Roll's half-brother Austrian School wins at Musselburgh in April 2019

Cakes sent to Gordon Elliott's yard from Godolphin, 'proud vendors of Tiger Roll', in April 2018

In the last year, I switched to 14 per cent pellets as somebody told me the crows won't eat the pellets, and they were right.

'I haven't manured the land since my dad died 26 years ago but limed it once. A friend runs a flock of sheep over it which greatly helps. I used to keep a few cattle, but they created too many divots.'

If anyone was not convinced of O'Brien's delight at breeding a winner of the most famous jumps race in the world when Classic success was the aim, his passionate defence of Tiger Roll in response to perceived slights about the horse's diminutive stature should put the case beyond doubt.

'Michael O'Leary's choice of the word "rat" to describe the horse is very much misplaced,' he says. 'Tiger is anything but. He is endowed with perfect conformation, balance and a unique presence. Indeed, he is an artist's dream to paint or sculpt.

'Northern Dancer and Lyric Fantasy, the "pocket rocket", were smaller than Tiger was and they were never denigrated by their owners, but rather extolled.'

O'Brien has the ultimate riposte to those who do not afford smaller horses the respect they deserve.

'Where were they when Tiger's half-brother Austrian School – a colossus, a giant – was sold for just 20,000gns at Tattersalls in October 2016? He's already a dual winner at two.'

Peter Thomas talked to all those associated with Tiger Roll after his success in the Grand National:

For all the tributes paid by the form book, for all the reverent words that will appear in due course in the annals of the turf, it's perhaps Gordon Elliott who best sums up the appeal of Tiger Roll. 'He's given great days to so many people,' says the man who has led him to all his finest hours, and he couldn't be more right, although perhaps even the trainer doesn't realise the vast reach of the joy that has been dispensed.

To Lisa O'Neill and Keith Donoghue, 'Tiger' gifted first winners at the Cheltenham Festival; to Michael O'Leary he has handed four glory days in the famous maroon and white; for Elliott it was a second Grand National that similarly delighted everybody at Cullentra House Stables and quite possibly across the whole of County Meath; Davy Russell's reward was worldwide public redemption in the saddle from which he was once unceremoniously ejected. But that's not all.

Sheikh Mohammed, so they say, when informed by telephone in the immediate aftermath that a horse of his had won the most famous race in the world, was at first bemused and then 'tickled pink' to be reminded of the underwhelming little colt who had passed through Godolphin's doors – both in and out – at the beginning of the decade. He laughed uproariously, apparently, to learn of the well-bred foal who had failed to make the grade at the most prestigious academy in the country, only to follow a circuitous path to fame on a different planet entirely.

If the distant laughter of the ruler of Dubai sounds not a little surreal, then it fits in perfectly with the rest of the tale of Tiger Roll, whose rise to the coveted position of 'the people's horse' has been nothing short of unbelievable. From unwanted son of a Derby winner to the hero of a racing nation is a mighty step for such a diminutive beast, but it's one he has taken in his stride.

The story begins with the consignment of Tipperary breeder Jerry O'Brien's product of a mating between Authorized and Swiss Roll, herself a daughter of Guineas winner Entrepreneur, himself a grandson of the great Sadler's Wells. Born in 2010, the product of this well-fated union was snapped up for 70,000gns at Tattersalls December Foals sale by John Ferguson on behalf of Sheikh Mohammed – but destiny, and a lack of obvious talent, decreed that his time with the organisation would be short.

'Broken in, slow to come to hand, gelded, sold,' is how Marie Sullivan, bloodstock sales manager at Godolphin, sums it up, succinctly but as nicely as possible. 'We bought him in his foaling year and then he moved over to Ballysheehan, one of our farms in Ireland, spent the remainder of his foal year and most of his yearling year there and then moved across to our pre-training facility down Hamilton Road in Newmarket.

'He was broken in there but didn't race for us. He just didn't show much and never went into training, but we cheered him on at Aintree, that's for sure. We're very proud here in the Godolphin sales division of having sold him and we enjoyed Cheltenham for three years and then like everybody else enjoyed the National and pretended we've played a bigger part in it than we actually have!'

Everywhere he goes, it seems, Tiger Roll is remembered with fondness. Even Nigel Hawke, the man who sold the three-time festival winner and Grand National god for a mere £80,000, remains full of admiration, but then it must help that he only paid £10,000 for him in the first place.

'I was at Chepstow on National day and nobody cheered him more than me,' says the Devon trainer, who bought Tiger Roll at Doncaster in August 2013 and trained him to a convincing juvenile hurdle success at Market Rasen – where he is soon to have a bar named after him – that November before cashing in his chips.

'It was a funny feeling after he crossed the winning line, thinking, "Bloody hell, did I let him go?", but it was still a great day. Where I feel I missed out was in the Triumph Hurdle because I always thought he could win it, but I'm not going to tell you I thought he'd win two more races at the festival and a Grand National, because that was never on our agenda.'

Hawke's 'smash-and-grab' yielded a profit of £70,000 that 'wasn't wasted' as investment in his business, and although he may harbour some nagging regrets about selling, he can take solace in being the first man to identify the true promise of a future icon.

'I remember I took him up to Cheltenham myself two or three days before the sales and I rode him every morning on the racetrack and he was an absolute saint,' he says. 'It was just me and that horse for three days and you get a bit of a bond, and he was just a lovely horse to do anything with.

'Everybody knocks his size but from day one he was absolutely brilliant at a jump. You watch him through the Grand National and he has an amazing eye for an obstacle, and he's never fallen, which tells you everything. We were thinking about juvenile hurdles not Nationals, so size wasn't an issue.'

Trainer Nigel Hawke sent Tiger Roll out to make a winning debut at Market Rasen in November 2013

Size didn't matter to Hawke and a lack of it hasn't hindered Tiger Roll, but it has become an issue thanks to his owner Michael O'Leary's unflattering assessment of the 'little rat of a thing' in the wake of his victory in the Cross Country Chase at Cheltenham. It was a soundbite straight out of the O'Leary handbook, guaranteed to raise a titter and an eyebrow, but it stuck in the minds of the media and has become a 'thing' in the public consciousness, although hopefully not an epitaph in years to come.

Certainly the description finds little favour with Eddie O'Leary, manager at his brother's Gigginstown House Stud, who helped bring the over-achieving rodent into the fold when Hawke decided to sell.

'When Michael says he's a little rat he's only talking off,' says Eddie, before offering a qualified compliment of his own. 'He's a wonderful, wonderful horse but I mean it with total respect when I say he's never been a good horse, not a classy horse who travels like an airplane. Of course he's a good horse, but he's not a "good horse".

'We thought he could be a Fred Winter type. We saw he'd been bought unraced from Darley and that Nigel hadn't had him long, so we thought we might be able to find a bit of improvement in him, but we never thought he was a Triumph horse.'

It seems Tiger Roll has to work hard for respect wherever he goes. Mags O'Toole, the bloodstock agent instrumental in picking him out at Brightwells' Cheltenham sale in December 2013, is happy to give credit where it's due, albeit with the usual caveats.

'He's the gift that keeps on giving,' she says. 'You'll find much better horses who don't achieve ten per cent of what he's done, but he turns up at every dogfight and gives his best.

'I thought he was a three or four-year-old hurdler and unlikely to go further down the road. He's only 15.2 hands and horses like that don't win cross-country races or four-mile chases, but his spirit has carried him this far.'

'He's a complete over-achiever with the heart of a lion,' concurs Eddie, 'but legends tend to get bigger and he seems to be getting smaller. Braveheart ended up 15ft tall but Tiger Roll will be a Thelwell pony by the time the story's finished if you believe what you read.

'He's not that small. He's a Flat horse and in among all those big chasing horses he can look a bit small, but he's a well-made, well-balanced horse and you admire his heart and his will to win, and if there's one thing you have to admire more than anything else it's his trainer, because Tiger Roll was made for Gordon Elliott.'

Except it seems that there was a time when Elliott was less than enamoured at having been sent 'the rat' to train. Gigginstown had bought another horse later in the day at Cheltenham, a strapping son of Scorpion who fetched a cool £290,000 and was top of the trainer's wish list – but that one ended up with Willie Mullins.

'I liked the other one, but I got stuck with Tiger Roll and I wasn't very happy,' confesses Elliott, by now soothed by the balm of success, 'but I got lucky and it worked out grand.'

The extent of the row between trainer and management at Gigginstown varies depending on whether you listen to the authorised or unauthorised version, but work out grand it certainly did, with Tiger Roll winning the Triumph on only his second start for the Cullentra House team, in the hands of Russell, who had been relieved of his role as number-one rider to Gigginstown just three months earlier.

That was as far as the planning process had gone. The horse had done what he was bought for and now it was time to look ahead, but Eddie O'Leary was encouraged by the fact the Triumph had become a trialling ground for a better class of hurdler.

'The Fred Winter has taken the cavalry charge out of the Triumph, and the winners have progressed into Champion Hurdle horses,' he says, 'so we thought great, we've got a Champion Hurdle horse. Then we went up to Down Royal in October thinking we'd win, and he was travelling great until the fourth-last, when he was pulled up with what we thought was a broken pelvis. He was absolutely sound by the time he got back to the stables, so I don't know what happened, but something fell off that day.'

'He didn't fracture or break anything but just went very wrong behind and it took us a long, long time to get him back and right,' explains Elliott. 'To be honest the future was looking bleak for him. He looked buggered and we didn't know if we were ever going to get him back right.

'We did it in the end but we knew he'd gone a bit slow, so we knew we were going to have to go chasing, so we did and he won a couple of novices and we decided the National Hunt Chase was going to be the way to go at the festival. He travelled for Lisa that day but he hit a few.'

Eddie O'Leary is rather more brutal in his assessment of that second festival success, achieved on his 13th chase run. 'He head-butted every fence at Cheltenham for four miles,' he recalls with incredulity. 'That evening Gordon said to me: "There's two races for him next year, the Cross Country Chase and the Aintree National." I said: "Gordon, he's after head butting every fence today; how's he going to get round those courses?"

'That man can see round corners, I tell you. That was the plan the whole year and there you go, boom-boom. The man is a genius.'

'He laughed at me when I told him what I wanted to do,' confirms Elliott, 'so it was great for them to let me do what I wanted to with him. I thought he seemed to like Cheltenham, which was a massive bonus, I liked the idea of coming back to the festival and that was the race he suited, so that was the road I went, the same as with Cause Of Causes (won the Cross Country and second in the National in 2017) and Silver Birch (second in the Cross Country and won the Grand National in 2007).

'If I told you I thought he was definitely going to win the National at the time, I'd be lying, but I thought Cheltenham would be a lovely stepping stone towards it.'

If this is the tale of an over-achieving racehorse, it's also emblematic of a turning of the tide in Irish jump racing with Tiger Roll playing his part in earning for Elliott the accolade of top trainer at this year's Cheltenham Festival, where he pipped Mullins 8-7, and for Gigginstown the accolade of leading owner.

Not that Tiger Roll has been concerned with the rivalry between Ireland's new 'big two'. His Grand National win, so nearly snatched from him on the run-in by Pleasant Company, was simply another remarkable chapter in the story of an unlikely hero with an uncommon knack of making the most of himself. He may not have

been bought as a 'good horse', but by God he's become something pretty close to one.

'You couldn't have predicted any of it,' concedes Eddie O'Leary, 'but he has the heart of a lion and that's the greatest thing about him. When he's done trying there are a lot of fellas by the wayside.'

A hero he may be, but Tiger Roll doesn't always wear a white hat at home. He can be a bad boy but his achievements mean he's afforded a degree of latitude.

'The girls will tell you he's a bit like a tiger at home,' reported Elliott when the horse returned a little tired and crotchety from his Aintree exertions. 'He can be in very good form or very bad. In fairness, he's allowed to be in bad form as much as he wants because he's a great horse.'

Louise Dunne, who looks after 'Tiger', confirmed: 'He's a star. He's grumpy, but very lovable – a little character. He'd let you know if he didn't want you in the stable. He's a funny, quirky horse, but he's lovely.'

The final word went to the trainer, who clearly believes lovely is as lovely does: 'He just wants to help you, he tries, he's a character,

Gordon Elliott, Anita O'Leary, Davy Russell and Michael O'Leary in the Aintree winner's enclosure

Mags O'Toole (left) collects Tiger Roll's Horse of the Year trophy from Alice Everitt at Sandown in April 2018

he doesn't always do everything straightforward but he's brilliant. He definitely wasn't bought to do what he's done but he's been awesome – and he's only eight.'

As the season drew to a close the votes for Horse of the Year were counted and the prizes were handed out on the final day at Sandown. Tiger Roll, unsurprisingly, picked up the big one and Alice Everitt was on to hand to report:

He may have held on to Grand National glory by a whisker, but Tiger Roll was voted the 2017-18 Racing Post Jumps Horse of the Year by a clear margin.

The highly versatile chaser, whose finest hour came this month when holding off a late charge from Pleasant Company to win the £1 million Aintree spectacular, was declared the winner at the end of season jumps awards at Sandown yesterday.

In a competition previously won by the likes of Sprinter Sacre, Many Clouds and Thistlecrack, *Racing Post* readers cast a record 4,355 votes, of which 1,929 were for Tiger Roll.

With owner Michael O'Leary at Punchestown, the award was accepted by bloodstock agent Mags O'Toole, who purchased Tiger Roll on behalf of Gigginstown in December 2013.

At just eight, Tiger Roll has already enjoyed a remarkable career. Aside from his Grand National heroics, he has three wins at the Cheltenham Festival to his name – in the Triumph Hurdle, National Hunt Chase and this year's Cross Country.

Second was emphatic Champion Chase winner Altior, who was to land the bet365 Celebration Chase on a day that witnessed four of the award nominees – Native River, Might Bite, Buveur D'Air and Politologue – parade in front of racegoers.

It was an outstanding season for Tiger Roll and being only eight meant there was the prospect of more to come. However, no one could possibly imagine what would happen at the climax to the 2018-19 season.

5
Festival four-timer

Following a sensational victory in the 2018 Grand National, Tiger Roll went on his summer holidays to his owner's stud in County Westmeath and in late June Eddie O'Leary gave an update on his progress:

He came back to Gigginstown after Punchestown and he's the kind of horse who's easy to deal with.

After a hard season he's like a child's pony and he takes no time to get into a new routine.

He'll be out day and night for six weeks, in for a feed, spend a little time on the walker, and then he'll be back out again.

He's very laid-back, out in a field with Samcro and a few more of them at the moment, getting fat – when they get too fat is when you start them back walking.

He'll be just on grass while he's here, with a few nuts, to clean out the system, then once he's had a good rest we'll ease him back into things and he'll go back to Gordon Elliott.

Tiger Roll (left) with Mengli Khan at Gigginstown House Stud in June 2018

Tiger Roll at Gigginstown House Stud

Hopefully a summer off will do him good and his programme next season will be the same as last time – the cross-country races and, with luck, back to the National – more of the same.

At the end of August Gordon Elliott confirmed that Tiger Roll was back in training and would be targeted at back-to-back wins in the Aintree showpiece.

'Tiger Roll's in great form, back cantering away,' he said, 'and the plan would be to start him off in a cross-country race at Cheltenham before Christmas. Everything went so well last season that there's no reason not to do all the same things again.'

Eddie O'Leary added: 'He has the heart of a lion and that's the most admirable thing about him. When he's done trying there are a lot of fellas by the wayside.'

The cross-country race at Cheltenham's November meeting was earmarked as the starting point for Tiger Roll where he was set to carry top weight of 11st 12lb. Elliott said: 'It's a big ask, but the cross-country race at the track in March is going to be his Gold Cup.'

It was indeed a big ask as Lee Mottershead reported:

You will not be surprised to learn that for Josies Orders the rest of this season will revolve around trying to supplement success in Cheltenham's November cross-country chase by winning the one staged over course and distance in March.

You may be more surprised to learn that same festival prize is also the prime aim for Tiger Roll, even more so than defending his Randox Health Grand National crown.

On this occasion Tiger Roll was a staying-on fourth at the end of a Glenfarclas-backed handicap the Enda Bolger-trained Josies Orders took despite being briefly headed by Fact Of The Matter just after the final fence. The winner will be back here in December and March, as will Tiger Roll, who by winning that event last term became a triple festival hero.

'The festival race will be more important than the National, to be honest,' said Tiger Roll's trainer Gordon Elliott.

'I would love to win at Aintree again, but he'll probably have top weight and you have to be realistic. It would be easier to win at the festival – and to win at the Cheltenham Festival four times would be a dream come true.'

Tiger Roll in action over Cheltenham's cross-country course in November 2018

Elliott added: 'I was delighted with him today. I loved the way he galloped from the last fence to the line. That's the most important thing. I thought I had him a bit fitter but Tiger must be getting cuter at home.'

No horses are cuter, smarter or more potent over Cheltenham's cross-country track than those trained by Bolger, whose latest winner here had taken the same race three years ago.

'He really knows his way around here and cuts the corners,' said Bolger, who was also full of praise for winning rider Mark Walsh, now the trainer's first-choice pilot for these centre-course marathons following the retirement of Nina Carberry.

'A lot of the professionals either love it or they don't,' said Bolger. 'There was a gap to be filled and Mark really enjoys these races.'

He really does.

'I've loved jumping banks and hedges so to race over them at Cheltenham is a dream come true,' said Walsh.

Tiger Roll may have been defeated, but Keith Donoghue was unconcerned as David Jennings reported:

Tiger Roll's jockey Keith Donoghue says Friday's Cheltenham comeback has set the tone for another successful season, with a return to the course next month very much on the agenda for the Grand National hero.

Giving 15lb to Josies Orders in Cheltenham's first cross-country race of the season proved a bridge too far for Tiger Roll but the way he picked up when reaching the racecourse proper thrilled Donoghue.

Donoghue said: 'This is not his time of year so for him to run the way he did was very encouraging. He had to give weight to everything and he won't have to do that in March.

'I'd say he is better than ever this season. That was a brilliant starting point and you will not see the best of him until March or April. That is when he comes alive every year.

'He was behind the bridle for a lot of the race at Cheltenham but he just came alive when he reached the racecourse and he flew home.

'He took a blow after the Canal Turn but took off with me once he got his second wind.

'He has been in great form at home but he would still have needed his first run like he always does. Gordon [Elliott] trains him with spring in mind. That is always his goal.'

He added: 'The plan is to come back next month for the cross-country race and then on to the festival in March. I cannot wait to get back on him again.

'He is such a thrill to ride, you have no idea what it feels like. He is a little legend.'

Donoghue was overwhelmed by racegoers clapping Tiger Roll back into the parade ring at Cheltenham.

He said: 'I couldn't believe it when I saw all the people coming over to the railings to clap him back to the parade ring after the race. I got a shock to be honest. I don't think I realised just how popular he is. They love him over at Cheltenham.'

Tiger Roll is generally 4-1 favourite to win the Glenfarclas Cross Country Chase at the festival, where he would be bidding for his fourth success in five years.

Tiger Roll was all set to run in the cross-country chase at Cheltenham's December meeting but stayed at home, not due to unsuitable ground or out of sympathy for the cheese wedges, but because of a reason Elliott explained with commendable honesty.

'I thought it was a conditions race,' said Elliott. 'Then I found out it wasn't and I didn't want him carrying top weight in a handicap. I'll give him one run over hurdles to open up his wind pipes and then he'll be back here for the festival. That's his Gold Cup.'

Meanwhile, Market Rasen opened a bar on Boxing Day named in honour of Tiger Roll to mark the occasion five years earlier when he made a winning debut at the course.

The track's general manager Nadia Powell said: 'We're delighted to be honouring the Randox Health Grand National winner Tiger Roll, whose career began at Market Rasen.'

At the end of January 2019 Jerry O'Brien collected the award for National Hunt achievement at the Irish Thoroughbred Breeders' Association's national breeding and racing awards.

Thoughts now turned to Aintree and a bid for a historic second Grand National triumph as David Carr reported in February:

Gordon Elliott threatened to write his old boss out of the record books as he revealed he could have more than a third of the field in the Randox Health Grand National on April 6. He is no stranger to running huge teams in big races in Ireland and 12 of his horses are guaranteed a place at Aintree, featuring in the top 40 when the weights were revealed yesterday.

The trainer also has another four chasers in the top 70 for the £1 million race, which has usually been high enough up the handicap to get a run in recent seasons.

The modern record for runners in the National is the ten sent out in 2001 by Martin Pipe, whose former amateur rider will field as many as he can in a bid to land a third Aintree triumph.

'I'll run as many as I can get in,' said Elliott. 'We've won it twice and we want to win it again. If I can get ten or 15 in there I'll run them.

'We're used to it going racing every day, I've got good staff working for me. It's the biggest steeplechase in the world, it's the

Jerry O'Brien (left) receives his National Hunt achievement award from John Osborne in January 2019

Tiger Roll exercises in the water with Davy Russell on board

race that everyone wants to win. We'll try to get them all there first but I'll run as many as I can.'

Tiger Roll emulated Elliott's Silver Birch by landing the National last year but will race off a mark 9lb higher 12 months on.

'Tiger Roll has a very hard task,' said the trainer. 'He has a lot more weight this year but we'll see what happens. He's going to run in the Boyne Hurdle on Sunday and then go to Cheltenham.

'It's going to be a struggle for him. I suppose his Gold Cup this year is going to be the cross-country race at Cheltenham and if he's back for the National, great. Whatever happens happens, he doesn't owe us anything.'

Elliott, who has 22 National entries, is happier with the weight handed to last year's Irish Grand National winner General Principle.

Tiger Roll added to his story with a marvellous victory in the Boyne Hurdle as Justin O'Hanlon reported:

Tiger Roll makes a winning return over the smaller obstacles in the Boyne Hurdle at Navan in February 2019

Tiger Roll has already proved himself a remarkable horse, with his victory in last season's Grand National augmenting three Cheltenham Festival successes over vastly divergent trips, but

A beaming Louise Dunne with Tiger Roll in the Navan winner's enclosure

another chapter of his tall tale was written with his almost effortless 25-1 success in the Grade 2 Ladbrokes Ireland Boyne Hurdle.

There is now a new favourite for the Randox Health Grand National in April, with Tiger Roll cut to 12-1 (from 20) to become the first since Red Rum in the 1970s to win back-to-back Nationals.

Hopes for a big run at Navan were probably not that high. He looked like a mare in foal in the parade ring and it was abundantly clear the race was likely to bring him on enormously. To therefore see him do what he did in the race was, well, remarkable.

It's questionable whether he has ever travelled as well through a race. He seemed to be doing little more than a half-speed for Keith Donoghue, and when he asked him to go and win his race he did so comfortably.

He drew away from second favourite Off You Go to score by four lengths, with stablemate Cracking Smart third and market leader Bachasson a disappointing fourth.

Next up is the Cross Country Chase at Cheltenham, which Tiger Roll won last year, and, if anything, is an ever bigger ambition for connections than landing a second National.

Tiger Roll with his delighted connections after the Boyne Hurdle

Tiger Roll is favourite for that too, and was cut into no bigger than 6-4 (from 2-1) with Betfred.

Trainer Gordon Elliott said: 'I thought he and Cracking Smart would have been second-last and last, so it's a nice surprise!

'The plan is to go for the Cross Country at Cheltenham now. He'll take a fair bit of beating with a clear round, and then hopefully we'll go for the Grand National again.

'He'll be Keith's ride in the Cross Country, but Davy Russell will ride him in the National if he wants to.'

Elliott added: 'He's a special horse, he's a favourite around the yard and everyone loves him. He has paid for himself now for the year once again. We put the blinkers back on today as he was getting a bit lazy at home. He'll improve plenty for this; I'd say he was only 75 per cent fit.'

Donoghue, who partnered Gigginstown's Tiger Roll to win the Cross Country last year, was riding his first winner since returning from an injury sustained at Limerick over Christmas.

He said: 'That was a serious performance. He needed the run a little bit but his class got him through. He was fresh and well and tanked through the race. Hopefully it's all systems go for Cheltenham now.'

NAVAN

February 17, 2019
Ladbrokes Ireland Boyne Hurdle
2m5f

1	Tiger Roll	Keith Donoghue	25-1
2	Off You Go	Mark Walsh	7-4
3	Cracking Smart	Jack Kennedy	11-2

4 lengths, 2¼ lengths
6 ran

RACING POST ANALYSIS – Alan Sweetman

Tiger Roll, making his second appearance since last season's Grand National triumph, produced a remarkable performance to win this readily on his first outing over hurdles since the 2016 Punchestown festival.

All the assumptions were that this was a warm-up for the Cross Country at Cheltenham en route to Aintree, but he could be called the probable winner from some way out. The former Triumph Hurdle winner has already been rightly hailed for the versatility of his overall career record, and this was a further demonstration of what a rare sort he is. Another Cheltenham Festival success must be a strong possibility and a second National not out of the question, even if history is against him.

Tiger Roll had played a major role in the career of Keith Donoghue and the jockey was keen to praise his old ally, as David Jennings explained:

Not only has Tiger Roll won at three Cheltenham Festivals and grabbed Grand National glory but he has also revived the career of

Keith Donoghue, who says he would not be where he is today but for the pint-sized superstar.

Donoghue was on board Tiger Roll for his shock 25-1 success in Sunday's Boyne Hurdle at Navan and will retain the ride when the pair try to defend their Glenfarclas Cross Country Chase crown next month.

Rewind two years and the talented rider was about to take a six-month sabbatical from the game he loves so much due to a constant, bruising battle with the scales.

Donoghue said yesterday: 'Tiger Roll has been absolutely brilliant for my career, he's put me back on the map. There's no way I'd be where I am now but for him.

'To have an association with a horse like him is massive for me. He's so famous now. We were clapped all the way into the winner's enclosure at Navan yesterday. That was an incredible feeling.

'He's a real crowd favourite and must be one of the most popular horses in training.'

He continued: 'About two years ago I took about five or six months out, but my weight has never been better than now. I did

Keith Donoghue salutes the crowd after winning the Boyne Hurdle on Tiger Roll

11st 3lb for Tiger Roll yesterday and managed to do 11st 2lb over Christmas. I'm able to eat properly too.

'I went for a run yesterday morning and then had a sweat, so it wasn't much torture at all.'

Tiger Roll is now the shortest-priced Irish-trained horse in festival ante-post markets at no bigger than 5-4 for the Cross Country, and Donoghue would not put any punters off despite such skimpy odds.

'He's actually better than ever,' added Donoghue. 'He was quite stuffy in the early part of the race so there's loads of improvement to come as well. I kept him wide to make sure he got a proper run and a good blowout. I didn't want to get hampered or brought down or anything like that.

'Then, when we swung out of the back straight, he came back hard on the bridle and I couldn't believe it. I was petrified I was going to get there too soon and Gordon would kill me, but it all worked out in the end. I cannot wait for March 13.'

Beyond Cheltenham, Tiger Roll is also favourite to win the Randox Health Grand National at no bigger than 12-1, and were he to do so he would be the first to win back-to-back Nationals since the legendary Red Rum in 1973-74.

Eye of the Tiger: at home in February 2019

First, though, Tiger Roll would spearhead Elliott's Cheltenham Festival team where the County Meath handler would also attempt to defend the leading trainers' title he had won in the previous two seasons.

Elliott had saddled 22 winners at the festival, 14 of those in the previous two years, underlining the enormous strides he had made since Chicago Grey gave him a first festival victory in the 2011 National Hunt Chase.

'Cheltenham is the meeting where all trainers want to do well,' he said.

'You can train plenty of winners at Aintree or Punchestown, but it's how you do at the Cheltenham Festival that people remember.

'We've been very lucky there in recent years. It's very hard to see us bettering last year's score, but we'll be going there with plenty of chances.'

Elliott said of Tiger Roll: 'I was completely surprised by him at Navan. I thought he might beat a few of his rivals but I never felt he would win.

'We were hoping he'd run well before heading for the Cross Country but what he did was absolutely amazing.

'He travelled, hurdled really well and ran away from them. It showed just how good and versatile he is.

'He's a great favourite with all the staff and he's come out of the race in good order.

'We're hoping he can add to his impressive festival record.'

Scott Burton looked back at Tiger Roll's festival record:

Tiger Roll works on the gallops at Cullentra House Stables with Simon McGonagle on board

Can a horse truly know the difference between an ordinary day's racing and the big occasion, when everything matters a great deal more? Can he or she be enlivened by the extra swathes of people, the louder sounds and perhaps the heightened nerves of the humans around them? If we're honest about it then the vast majority probably have little idea but there are surely exceptions and if not, how else do you explain the career of Tiger Roll? Three-time Cheltenham Festival winners are still rare enough, even in the era of the 28-race carnival.

But to win a Triumph Hurdle, a National Hunt Chase and then the Cross Country – three utterly divergent tests of a horse – across four visits to the festival, before topping it off with success in the Grand National, takes a horse of great versatility and no small amount of talent.

Lisa O'Neill exercises Tiger Roll at Cheltenham in March 2019

Such great days have ensured the 'failed' Flat-bred has an enormous public following, while he has brought untold joy to the staff at Gordon Elliott's Cullentra House stable and his owners, Michael and Eddie O'Leary's Gigginstown House Stud.

But it's worth remembering that, away from the bright lights, Tiger Roll has finished out of the money on 14 of his 33 career starts.

Each handbrake turn in his career has come because Elliott appeared to have run out of options with a horse who was bought only as a juvenile hurdling prospect and whose career has looked to be on the wane more than once.

Elliott has a distinctive way of telling the Tiger Roll story, his rapid delivery lending a sense of inevitability to what on the face of it is a most unlikely tale.

'Eddie O'Leary and Mags O'Toole liked the look of him and bought him for £80,000 at Brightwells Cheltenham sale one month after his win for Nigel Hawke. He ran only once for us before winning the Triumph.

'He pulled up lame at Down Royal in October 2014 and although he came back and ran in Graded races, including a few Grade 1s, he made little impact and seemed to lack the speed required.

'We decided to send him over fences and he won his first two starts but, as time went on, it began to look as if he needed plenty of distance and that proved to be the case when he won the four-miler at Cheltenham in 2017.

'He lost his way a bit after that and we decided to try something new and go down the cross-country route. That paid off at Cheltenham last year and he surpassed everything else by going on to win the Grand National.'

Each of those three festival triumphs came under a different rider but there is a golden thread which runs through them: the sight of Tiger Roll travelling just in behind the leaders with almost laughable ease.

The 2014 Triumph under Davy Russell appeared straightforward enough in the run, the first evidence that Tiger Roll has a fine cruising speed when allowed to find his own rhythm.

The National Hunt Chase is twice the distance of the Triumph Hurdle and, along with the Cross Country Chase, can generally be relied on for its unhurried, un-festival pace early on.

In the four-miler, under a beautiful steer from Lisa O'Neill – who passed up three shuddering opportunities to sever the partnership – and again with Keith Donoghue in last year's Cross Country, Tiger

Previous spread: Keith Donoghue holds on tight
as Tiger Roll clears the water jump in the Cross
Country Chase at Cheltenham in March 2019

4.10 RACE 5
Glenfarclas Chase (A Cross Country Chase) (Class 2)
ITV
Winner £40,235 (3m 6f 37y) **3m6f X-Country**

£65,000 guaranteed **For** 5yo+ **Weights** 5yo 11st 2lb; 6yo+ 11st 4lb **Allowances** mares 7lb **Entries** 20 pay £90 **Confirmed** 20 pay £235.00 **Penalty value 1st** £40,235 **2nd** £11,947 **3rd** £5,973.50 **4th** £2,977 **5th** £1,495 **6th** £754 **7th** £377 **8th** £182

1 -12B3F1 **AUVERGNAT** (FR) [31] S6
b g Della Francesca-Hesmeralda
E Bolger (IRE)   John P McManus
8 11-4
Mark Walsh
(158)

2 5511-19 **BEEVES** (IRE) [283] (38H) S3 F1
b g Portrait Gallery-Camas North
Jennie Candlish   Paul & Clare Rooney
b 11 11-4
Sean Quinlan
(162)

3 226-PP1 **BLESS THE WINGS** (IRE) [89] S1 C1 CD1
b g Winged Love-Silva Venture
Gordon Elliott (IRE)   Adrian Butler/S P O'Connor
p 13 11-4
Davy Russell
(162)

4 232-042 **CANTLOW** (IRE) [89] S3 F1 CD1
b g Kayf Tara-Winnowing
E Bolger (IRE)   John P McManus
p 13 11-4
Donal McInerney
(160)

5 P0512-0 **CAUSE OF CAUSES** (USA) [38] S3 C2 CD1
b g Dynaformer-Angel In My Heart
Gordon Elliott (IRE)   John P McManus
tp 10 11-4
Mr J J Codd
(168)

6 34417-3 **CHIC NAME** (FR) [31]
b g Nickname-Vuelta Al Ruedo
Richard Hobson   The Boom Syndicate
h 6 11-4
Jonathan Burke
(146)

7 -514553 **FEDERICI** [21] S3
b g Overbury-Vado Via
Donald McCain   Jon Glews
p 9 11-4
Will Kennedy
(146)

8 -401104 **HURRICANE DARWIN** (IRE) [31] S2
b g Westerner-Poetics Girl
Alan Fleming (IRE)   Barry Connell
t 8 11-4
Denis O'Regan
(144)

9 0-62302 **JOSIES ORDERS** (IRE) [31] S2 CD3
b g Milan-Silent Orders
E Bolger (IRE)   John P McManus
p 10 11-4
Ms N Carberry
(160)

10 53F23-P **SAINT ARE** (FR) [340] (46H)
b/br g Network-Fortanea
Tom George   D W Fox
tp 12 11-4
A P Heskin
(161)

11 320-224 **THE LAST SAMURI** (IRE) [46] S5
ch g Flemensfirth-Howaboutthis
Kim Bailey   Paul & Clare Rooney
10 11-4
David Bass
(173)

12 31P-2P5 **TIGER ROLL** (IRE) [89] S1 C3
b g Authorized-Swiss Roll
Gordon Elliott (IRE)   Gigginstown House Stud
tp 8 11-4
Keith Donoghue
(165)

13 7351-23 **URGENT DE GREGAINE** (FR) [117] S1 F1 CD1
b g Truth Or Dare I-Hispanie
Emmanuel Clayeux (FR)   Arnaud Rasquier
tp 10 11-4
Felix de Giles
(157)

14 3-13P22 **URUMQI** (FR) [24] S2
b g Soldier Of Fortune-Love In Paradise
D Cottin (FR)   Ecurie De Roebeck
t 7 11-4
Jonathan Plouganou
(140)

15 1481312 **VICOMTE DU SEUIL** (FR) [117] S7
b g Special Kaldoun-Marie Du Seuil
Emmanuel Clayeux (FR)   Mrs M Boudot
tp 9 11-4
Charlie Deutsch
(149)

16 -F63327 **BELAMIX DOR** (FR) [40]
b m Al Namix-Paladoune
Patrice Quinton (FR)   Ecurie Du Haras D'Erable
t 7 10-11
Thomas Beaurain
(136)

2017 (16 ran) **Cause Of Causes** Gordon Elliott 9 11-4 4/1   Mr J J Codd RPR158

BETTING FORECAST: 11-4 Cause Of Causes, 5 Tiger Roll, 11-2 The Last Samuri, 6 Josies Orders, 7 Auvergnat, 9 Bless The Wings, 14 Urgent de Gregaine, 20 Cantlow, 25 Hurricane Darwin, 33 Beeves, Saint Are, Vicomte Du Seuil, 40 Federici, Urumqi, 50 Belamix Dor, 66 Chic Name.

Roll simply enjoyed running away under his jockeys without the threat of being taken out of his comfort zone.

Usually the first thing anyone points out about Tiger Roll is that he looks so small against the strapping ex-stores he routinely encounters over such marathon trips.

Elliott wouldn't disagree: 'He's far from being the biggest horse in the world but he is a very accurate jumper, although he can get quite low at his fences. That being said he's never fallen and unseated his rider only once.'

It could just be we have all been making too big a deal of his size, notably since Michael O'Leary called him 'a rat of a thing' in the aftermath of his second Cheltenham success.

Because what comes back again and again from those three wins – not to mention his Aintree triumph – is the way he goes through a race.

Training racehorses is about bringing the athlete to a physical peak. But there is also an element of the psychoanalyst in the best practitioners.

Elliott says: 'He can be a bit of a character around the yard but he's a big favourite with all our staff. He's been quite straightforward to train.'

At several stages earlier in his career, Tiger Roll offered the chance for connections to throw their hands in the air.

But Elliott has taken it as a challenge to keep finding different ways to make him fall back in love with being a racehorse. And let's face it, spring is for lovers.

Tiger Roll showed he was a modern-day festival great as James Stevens reported:

Tiger Roll inspired a colossal roar from the Cheltenham crowd after an exemplary jumping display led him to a fourth festival victory in the Glenfarclas Cross Country Chase.

Keith Donoghue did not move out of second gear aboard last season's Grand National hero, who jumped perfectly over the 32 obstacles, effortlessly moving into the lead before the last and forging clear for a 22-length procession over Josies Orders.

The Gordon Elliott-trained star was given another enormous cheer as he returned to the winner's enclosure. He had previously landed the 2014 Triumph Hurdle and the 2017 National Hunt Chase, and has now won the past two runnings of this unique contest at the festival.

Elliott, who secured his first victory at this year's meeting and made it two with Envoi Allen in the bumper, said: 'It was brilliant,

he looked very good. He jumped and just did everything right. Keith has a great relationship with the horse.

'He's won at four Cheltenham Festivals and a Grand National as well, so he's a very special horse. He looked as good as he's ever been, he was unbelievable and I feel very lucky to have him.'

The popular nine-year-old, owned by Gigginstown House Stud, was cut to 5-1 to become only the second horse to repeat a Grand National success – a feat achieved only by the great Red Rum.

Elliott added: 'He'll go to the Grand National next. It's a big ask to win it again, he's 9lb higher, but we'll enjoy what he did today as it was brilliant.

'Of course we want to win the National again, but he's won at four Cheltenham Festivals, that's just incredible.'

Speaking later, Gigginstown's Eddie O'Leary confirmed the National as the plan, after an interview brother Michael gave suggesting there was an element of doubt.

The result signalled a turn in fortunes for Elliott who had seen well-fancied chances Hardline, Apple's Jade, Battleoverdoyen and Delta Work beaten at this year's festival.

'Everyone knows it's been a rough week,' said Elliott. 'Horses haven't been running up to par and some of them haven't been good enough. We're lucky to have a good bunch of horses and owners and we've kept going.'

CHELTENHAM
March 13, 2019
Glenfarclas Chase (A Cross Country Chase)
3m6f

1	Tiger Roll	Keith Donoghue	5-4f
2	Josies Orders	Mark Walsh	15-2
3	Urgent De Gregaine	Felix de Giles	17-2

22 lengths, ¾ length
15 ran

RACING POST ANALYSIS – David Toft

A race for course specialists and the early pace was generous. It saw a legend come home in glorious isolation.

Tiger Roll won this last year before going on to land the Grand National and he warmed up for his repeat bid here by landing a Grade 2 hurdle recently.

Never far from the front, he took it up some way out and absolutely bolted up, gaining a fourth win from five visits to this festival. Some bookmakers made him as short as 5-1 for the Aintree feature next month.

Keith Donoghue was thrilled with Tiger Roll's performance as David Jennings reported:

On this day two years ago Keith Donoghue weighed 12 and a half stone.

He was in his local pub watching Labaik, the headbanger he'd counselled in rehab for months, take off at the same time as everything else in the Supreme, much to everyone's amazement.

Not only that, but he flew home to give Jack Kennedy his first Cheltenham Festival winner. It should have been Donoghue.

The 25-year-old, in his typically honest way, reflects: 'I was done. That was it. My career was over. I didn't want to see another horse again.'

Fast-forward 730 days and Donoghue wakes up at 6.30am weighing 11st 3lb. He is tacking up Tiger Roll at 6.45am and the pair head out on to the track for a trot.

Donoghue tells me: 'He's bucking and kicking and acting the lad – that's definitely a good sign. He has his game face on.'

Once the second lot of Gordon Elliott's is put through their paces, it's time for breakfast. Well, it should be breakfast time, but Donoghue doesn't do breakfast, or lunch, or dinner, and hasn't done so since Monday morning.

He says: 'I haven't eaten anything today. Oh, actually, I had two pieces of white pudding. The lads in the house were eating a fry-up this morning so I robbed two small bits of pudding off them. That was it.

'I had two eggs and a piece of bacon Monday morning. That was the last proper meal I've had. I've drunk loads and loads of water, and once you're hydrated you're fine.

'I don't even feel like eating. This time last year I couldn't even drink water as I had to lose 7lb in a couple of hours.'

It's now 1.15pm and Donoghue is talking to me in a towel at the back entrance to the weighing room. He has had a power sweat, just 25 minutes or so, to get rid of 2lb.

He says: 'This is far more enjoyable when you don't have to worry about your weight too much. Last year I spent the whole day worrying about whether I'd make the weight or not.

'It wasn't enjoyable at all. I was petrified I wouldn't get down to the weight I needed to be. I couldn't enjoy it.

'I didn't even have to go running today as my weight is actually good. I haven't run since Monday. I ran six miles on Monday. I did the full cross-country course, then a lap of the main track.'

So, what's the plan with Tiger Roll?

'I'll try to ride him the same way I did last year,' comes the reply. 'Sit fourth, fifth or sixth and try to pick them off one by one and hope for the best.'

Keith Donoghue is congratulated by owner Michael O'Leary as he returns to the Cheltenham winner's enclosure on Tiger Roll

As the crowd are in awe of Altior, who gets punters back on the straight and narrow, Donoghue hands Elliott the saddle. It has so far been a torrid week for the trainer, whose face has now been drained of all colour.

'It's all up to you now, Jacksie [Donoghue's nickname],' says Elliott, who is still searching for his first winner of the week. He has already had four favourites beaten. No pressure, Keith.

This Donoghue chap doesn't do pressure, though. He is like a heavily sedated James Milner. He sticks to the script too. Starts off sixth, then fifth, fourth, third, second and, with five to jump there is nothing he can do but take it up. Tiger Roll has run three and a half miles and he's begging for more, pleading to go faster.

'I gave him a squeeze coming down the hill and he just took off with me,' reflects his rider. 'I had no idea how far clear I was, so I just took a sneak peak at the big screen to check. It was all over. All I had to do was get over the last. It's an incredible feeling coming up the hill at Cheltenham when you're so far clear.'

Tiger Roll wins by 22 lengths. Unlike when he won the race last year and finished knackered, the pint-sized pocket rocket has more than enough energy to bring his rider back down the chute and into the winner's enclosure.

'I know I said last year it didn't matter I walked back on my own, but it's a magic feeling coming back on the horse,' he admits.

'When you're walking down the chute you see so many familiar faces. Friends from home, the likes of Colm, Felim and Paddy O'Rourke, great friends of mine.'

And so what about Tiger Roll, then?

Donoghue answers: 'He's some little legend, isn't he? He's put me back on the map. People know my name now, when nobody knew who I was a few years ago. That's down to Gordon as well. He's not only a brilliant trainer but he's such a decent human being too. He stuck by me when others wouldn't. There's no way I'd be here today but for him.'

There will be some celebrations, surely?

'I don't drink, I've never even tasted alcohol, but I might go mad tonight and drink Coke instead of water,' says Donoghue.

Seldom has a soft drink been so richly deserved.

It was a memorable day for everyone at Cheltenham with the mighty Altior winning a second Champion Chase as Alastair Down reported:

Feel free to file me under 'senses taken leave of' but for all Altior's lordly magnificence he was equalled, and possibly even upstaged yesterday, by the extraordinary pocket phenomenon that is Tiger Roll.

Here is a horse whom the public have come to worship just this side of idolatry. Altior is pure brilliance as his unbeaten run of 18 victories testifies, an aristocrat of a racehorse.

But Tiger Roll is pure rock 'n' roll, a hero of humble origins whom you cannot help but love.

This was festival victory number four. He warmed up for this second Cross Country when winning a Grade 2 hurdle easily at Navan when he was 25-1 and had a tummy like a Dublin publican who never pours a pint of Guinness without having a glass himself. Just for quality control purposes, you understand.

Following spread: Tiger Roll (third left) clears the first obstacle

Louise Dunne can't bear to watch Tiger Roll

Altior looked as if he might be derailed coming to the last but his class is melded to an admirable adherence to that famous old Second World War maxim, 'Dig For Victory'.

And dig was exactly what he had to do – wresting back his second two-mile crown that had looked momentarily uneasy on his head.

When he returned it was the first time this week that every vantage point was taken around the winner's enclosure and he received a mighty reception.

But it was as nothing in comparison to the contagious eruption of noise that came at the point Tiger Roll took the lead five out in the Cross Country. Frankly, he was just showing off, all but hamming it up by leading so early. But he was clear two out and that gave the stands, lawn and even those in the posh seats the chance to revel in the sheer magnificence of the moment.

And revel we did. The racecourse simply exploded, blasting out that old black magic of heartfelt acclaim. It wasn't because he was favourite, the roar was born from the fact that he has become one of our all-time favourites.

His festival record is absurdly magical; then there is the small matter of a Grand National victory to throw into this story of the best 80 grand ever spent at a sale of the racehorse.

The last horse to land the National and go on to win at the festival the following year was Golden Miller, hero of five Gold Cups, back in 1935.

Golden Miller won the National but mostly loathed Aintree. Next month, if Tiger Roll returns to Aintree, he will just say, 'Oh, this place again. I'll give it a go.'

Connoisseurs of weird coincidences might like to know that Tiger Roll was foaled on March 14 and his Triumph, four-miler and last year's Cross Country were all landed on his birthday. Yesterday, he was a day early as it was the 13th, he was 13 on the card and his Aintree saddle cloth carried 13 as well.

Of such trivia are pub quizzes made.

Needless to say, Tiger Roll's return down the horsewalk was a cacophony of whoops, cheers and acclamatory madness. Minutes earlier, as he thundered up the hill from the last, we had experienced the first print blizzard of the week as endless newspapers were hurled skyward.

One of the special aspects of his triumphant progress into the winner's enclosure was that it was a case of justice delayed. Last year Tiger Roll got a touch of the staggers when pulling up and did not return to the holy ground beneath the steppings. So there were no photos of a lifetime for Keith Donoghue to savour.

Well, Tiger Roll has put that wrong to rights. Donoghue lives a couple of miles from Fairyhouse – you should have no trouble finding the house as it will be the only one covered entirely in pictures of the Cheltenham winner.

There is something almost Churchillian about Tiger Roll's bulldog spirit. Nothing fazes him, no challenge is too much. He is Mr Can Do or give it a bloody good try.

The gathering here is driven by a shared desire to see the great horses and relish their greatness. There is a camaraderie in that, something that cuts across all the boundaries the wider world erects to keep people apart.

And yes, Altior took us to the mountaintop and thank the Lord and N Henderson for him. Nico de Boinville reflected that 'the crowd are warming to him'.

That is rightly true, though the forged link is not yet as strong as that felt for his immediate Seven Barrows predecessor, Sprinter Sacre, who was on parade here in the morning in front of his unwavering fan base.

It's not Altior's fault he's not yet on that higher plane of affection; it's because we all suffered for Sprinter's art. He had many a sea of trouble to overcome – irregular heartbeats, more wind issues than a weather forecaster and plenty of other assorted ailments.

And, of course, he overcame the lot, which is why the Cleeve Hill mob cleaved to him.

Altior is undoubtedly a wonder. But greatness comes in humbler forms and that is why Tiger Roll has got under our skin to a degree that is palpable.

There is something all but redemptive about watching the scrapper chuck his heart ahead of him, stick his head down and gallop with every sinew straining in pursuit of that very great heart.

Altior and Tiger Roll. What a shining day – Cheltenham hot to the touch and every soul on course basking in the warmth of this place like no other.

Now it was time for Tiger Roll's bid for a place in the record books.

6
Aintree legend

After his fourth festival success Tiger Roll was shortened to a general 6-1 chance to claim back-to-back victories in the Grand National, but Eddie O'Leary warned that a decison wouldn't be made on his participation until closer to the time.

'Tiger Roll is an absolute superstar and we were delighted with him in the Cross Country,' said O'Leary. 'We haven't even begun thinking about what we'll do with him next, but I know Michael is concerned about what's best for the horse.

'Hopefully, if everything goes to plan, we'll go back to Aintree for the Grand National but we'll just wait and see with him.'

Reflecting on Gigginstown's Cheltenham, O'Leary added: 'We didn't have a bad week at all. We had seven winners last year when the ball bounced in our favour and we knew that would never happen for us again.

'We were aiming for one winner and we got it so we're absolutely thrilled. We had three seconds, five thirds and a lot of the horses ran well, which was great.'

Tom Peacock then spoke to bloodstock agent Mags O'Toole about how Gigginstown acquired Tiger Roll:

Tiger Roll has established himself in National Hunt folklore as the pint-size terrier with an infinite capacity to surprise and it is an asset which has even filtered down to the agent who bought him.

Mags O'Toole, who works closely with Michael and Eddie O'Leary's Gigginstown operation, acquired the equine polymath for what now seems an absolute steal at £80,000 as a three-year-old at Cheltenham in December 2013.

A son of Authorized, he had originally been bought for 70,000gns as a foal destined for a career on the Flat with Godolphin but had ended up juvenile hurdling with Nigel Hawke, scoring on his debut at Market Rasen three days before that sale.

Mags O'Toole with Gordon Elliott at
Cheltenham in March 2018

'An ex-Flat horse who had only had one run wouldn't really be the sort of thing Gigginstown would be looking for but it was a year when they didn't have a three-year-old hurdler/Triumph Hurdle horse and that's why he fell into the basket,' O'Toole explained.

'Eddie decides everything and does a brilliant job, you just go to a sale and see if there's something you like.

'He also wasn't the typical Gigginstown horse in that he's a small horse, as has been very well documented, but he'd won his only start, he jumped very well and had no mileage on the clock.

'Although he wasn't huge he was a very good-looking horse with a great action, and that's the sort of thing that Eddie would always head for.'

O'Toole's transaction followed that particular brief to the letter as, after running second in a Leopardstown Grade 1 on his introduction for Gordon Elliott, he swept the Triumph Hurdle up that March.

Adding on three more Cheltenham Festival wins and a certain event at Aintree, Tiger Roll's contribution is now more than £860,000.

'We never thought at the time "why don't we buy him, he could be a National horse one day",' O'Toole said, with permissible conviction.

'Hindsight is a very precise science isn't it? He's looked after everybody all his life, that little horse. Nigel Hawke bought him for £10,000 and took 80 for him that night, and that's a pretty fair return for any horse. And we bought him for 80 and when he won a Triumph Hurdle, we thought he had repaid us ten times over doing that, not knowing we were only starting out with him.'

The exact finances to those at the top end of the jumps are largely immaterial and Tiger Roll's contribution spreads much further.

He must now be the most popular character from the hundreds that both Gigginstown and Elliott have dealt with, with his 22-length virtuoso performance in Wednesday's Glenfarclas Cross Country Chase only enhancing his reputation further.

It was, unusually, the sole victory of the 2019 meeting in the maroon livery with ten others making the frame.

Although the agent's job has long been done, she too remains an ardent admirer.

'I adore him, how could you not?' O'Toole said. 'He's a feisty little fellow. I wouldn't be around the yard much but he lets you know when he's in good humour or not good humour because he'd kick out or he'd put his ears back. That's always a good sign and means he's on song.

'There's a good bit of fight in that horse, as you could well see at Aintree.

'He was like a motorbike going around Cheltenham. You wouldn't know what race he could have run in but they like to stick with where he might win and last year [the Cross Country] brought new life into him.

'I think he thought "this is fun, these fences are different", and I think when he got to Aintree he thought "this is quite good fun again". He's a marvellous, marvellous horse.'

The Tiger Roll bandwagon continued to pick up speed after Cheltenham as both the bookmakers and the handicapper reacted to his latest festival victory as Brian Sheerin reported:

Bookmakers yesterday predicted victory for Tiger Roll in the Randox Health Grand National would be their worst in the history of the race and they were given no comfort by the official handicapper who described last year's Aintree hero as being '8lb well in'.

BHA senior handicapper Martin Greenwood has raised Tiger Roll's official rating by that amount after his Cheltenham Festival win and admitted that might even be a conservative figure.

His assessment only heightened the confidence of trainer Gordon Elliott, who cut the image of a proud father as Tiger Roll led his string on the Cullentra gallops yesterday morning and confirmed the modern-day phenomenon would bid to become the first horse since Red Rum to win back-to-back Grand Nationals.

After Tiger Roll's Cross Country success at Cheltenham owner Michael O'Leary had expressed doubts about his participation at Aintree.

But speaking at the launch of the BoyleSports Irish Grand National, for which Tiger Roll was also handed an entry, Elliott admitted the world famous chase on April 6 at Aintree was very much plan A for a horse he believed was in even finer fettle than when winning the race by a head from Pleasant Company 12 months ago.

Elliott said: 'He's come out of Cheltenham very well and the plan is to go for the National. Obviously I'll have to discuss it with Eddie and Michael [O'Leary] but I can't see any reason why he won't be running there next.

'I spoke to the English handicapper yesterday and he said he put him up 8lb for winning the Cross Country, and he might have been easy on him giving him that, as he could have put him up 10lb or more. But, because it was the Cross Country race, he only put him up 8lb.'

And in an ominous warning for Tiger Roll's Aintree opponents, he added: 'It looks like he's a different horse this year than he was last year.'

Greenwood said: 'Tiger Roll has looked an even better horse since his break, sluicing up over hurdles at Navan before barely coming off the bridle in last week's Cross Country at Cheltenham. Tiger Roll's new mark is now 167, which may still be underestimating him.

'Obviously Tiger Roll will run off his early-closing mark of 159 in the National, which makes him 8lb well in.'

Tiger Roll could go off the shortest-priced National favourite since Hedgehunter and Clan Royal started at 5-1 in 2006.

Nicola McGeady of Ladbrokes, who have him priced at 5-1, said: 'Tiger Roll fever has hit punters as he looks to follow in the footsteps of Red Rum. He has made the day for punters time and time again, and if he completes the Grand National double we believe it will be the worst result in the history of the race for bookmakers.'

The gamble on Tiger Roll continued and layers feared that he would become the shortest-priced National winner in history, eclipsing 11-4 shot Poethlyn, who won the race in 1919.

A week before Aintree David Jennings looked back at Tiger Roll's career:

It says something when the biggest rock star in town can't even headline his own Cheltenham concert and is instead forced to do a duet with an act who couldn't sell a record while he was belting out his first number-one single in 2016.

The week after Altior won the best Supreme Novices' Hurdle in recent memory, Tiger Roll was second in an all-weather maiden at Dundalk, beaten by a rival rated 62 who has won just one race since.

Fast forward three years and Altior wins a second Champion Chase to supplement his Supreme success and Arkle victory, but the record Cheltenham crowd gives just as raucous a reception to Tiger Roll after he gallops to a 22-length triumph in the Glenfarclas Cross Country Chase.

So how has a tiny thoroughbred, so small his owner Michael O'Leary famously referred to him as a 'little rat', turned into one of the most popular horses in training? Perhaps it is because he has won at four Cheltenham Festivals, or maybe it is down to the fact his size could not prevent him from soaring over 29 fences (Becher's having been bypassed on the second circuit) on the way to landing last year's Grand National, or it could be his never-say-die attitude which helped him cling on narrowly when Pleasant Company lunged late at Aintree.

If you haven't fallen for Tiger Roll yet, you have a strange taste in thoroughbreds.

'He's a horse of a lifetime, an unbelievable horse. It looks like he's a different horse this year than he was last year,' says his trainer Gordon Elliott, who deserves enormous credit for turning a frustrated hurdler stuck in no-man's land into a top-class chaser.

Going further back, of course, it was Nigel Hawke who bought Tiger Roll for just £10,000 and sold him four months later for £80,000. A £70,000 profit looked like brilliant business by Hawke. Time has taken the gloss off it, however.

'It looked like the best piece of business I've ever done. He was bought to be sold on and it looked like great business. We were thrilled,' Hawke says.

'It's funny – if he didn't sell at Cheltenham he was going to run on the Saturday, so I spent three full days with him. I rode him out every morning and I actually fell in love with him. I got very attached to him. He was a pleasure to do anything with.'

The trainer adds: 'I actually thought he might win the Fred Winter that year. If they got him nicely handicapped, I thought he was an ideal Fred Winter type. I would be lying if I said I thought he would win four races at Cheltenham.

'He was a good work horse, but nothing special. He went through the motions, but he was always an exceptionally good jumper.'

It's fair to say Tiger Roll did not scream future Grand National winner.

Hawke says: 'I didn't think he would get around in the National last year; I wasn't quite sure he was man enough for Aintree. Boy did he prove me wrong!

'He has turned into a freak of nature. He's been absolutely amazing for racing and I feel very privileged to have been associated with him in my own little way.'

Tiger Roll may now be feted a National hero, but did you know this pint-sized pocket rocket is a bit of a diva? Louise Dunne is in a better position than anyone to describe Tiger Roll's personality and she says he craves carrots and attention more than anything.

Dunne, who is the mother of two sets of twins aged eight and six, has noticed a difference in Tiger Roll this season. He is not the horse he used to be – he is better.

'He's so grumpy but he's so lovable. He loves his carrots and he absolutely adores attention. I suppose you could say he's a bit of a diva,' Dunne says.

She adds: 'There's something about him over the last few months. He's all business now. He's more focused than I've ever seen him before. He wants to show everyone he's the boss every day now.'

And how are the nerves?

'Terrible,' she laughs. 'It's worse this year because there's so much hype about him, but rightly so. He deserves all the hype he's getting. He's absolutely amazing. Once he comes back safe and sound, I'll be happy.'

Too small, too short, too scrawny, not sexy enough. You need a certain type of horse to win the Grand National and Tiger Roll did not appear to be it when lining up in April 2018. Aintree was not a place for horses like him.

How wrong we were. Tiger Roll relished the challenge. Under a typically cool Davy Russell ride, the 10-1 shot started in mid-division but began to pick them off one by one heading out on to the final circuit. By the second-last it was blatantly obvious he was travelling better than anything else.

After safely popping over the 29th and final fence, it was not a case of if he won, but a case of how far. If you were told the winning distance would be a head, you wouldn't have believed them.

Elliott recalls: 'About 200 yards out I thought he was home and hosed. I was sure he was going to hack up.

'He's only small, though, so four miles and two and a half furlongs was going to be tough on him. In the last 100 yards he hit a brick wall, but thank God the line came in time. He's been a super little horse. I'm very proud of him.'

Here's hoping we all have cause to be proud of him again on Saturday.

As the big day approached comparisons were being made with Red Rum as David Baxter explained:

Should Tiger Roll justify favouritism and win Saturday's Randox Health Grand National he would be the first back-to-back winner since the legendary Red Rum in 1974.

Trained by the late Ginger McCain, Red Rum's feat has stood the test of time, but following a dominant performance in the Cross Country Chase at the Cheltenham Festival, punters and bookmakers feel Tiger Roll has an outstanding chance of matching the achievement.

McCain's son Donald himself triumphed with Ballabriggs in 2011, and while he rates Tiger Roll's chances of succeeding again highly, he does not think the achievements can be compared directly.

'I think Tiger Roll has a great chance of winning another National, and Gordon [Elliott] is making a fantastic job of him,' McCain said yesterday.

'But in regards of emulating Red Rum, and I know I'm a little bit biased, that ship has sailed.'

Red Rum (8) won the Grand National three times in 1973, 1974 and 1977

In the 40-plus years since Red Rum won his three Grand Nationals the race has undergone significant changes, including making the course and fences safer, along with how the race is formed from a handicapping perspective with the compressed weights.

Such alterations, McCain believes, make the Aintree marathon a very different test in the modern era, and he added: 'You didn't get 9lb for winning a Grand National in those days, you went from 10st 5lb to 12st and carried top weight every year afterwards.

'You were giving two stone to horses and weight to Gold Cup winners. The race has changed completely and I find it a little mind-boggling every year that a Grand National winner can go up 7lb or 9lb, and I've had one of those as well.

'It doesn't seem like the Aintree factor comes into winners somehow. The modern-day Grand National is a good-quality staying handicap chase, but the other factors have been taken out of it a bit.'

McCain does think Tiger Roll has a lot in his favour ahead of his National defence, and said: 'He's been trained for the day and I imagine the Cross Country will have put him spot on. If anybody can get the job done, Gordon can.

'If Tiger Roll can go and win a second Grand National it would be a feat that's not been done for many years and it might be a long time before it is done again in the modern era, but the race and the conditions have changed beyond recognition compared to those [Red Rum's] days.'

Tiger Roll emulated Red Rum to earn a place in racing legend as Lee Mottershead reported:

His place in racing history had long since been assured. Now the hearts and minds of all who love this sport will forever hold dear the tiny miracle that is Tiger Roll, after he followed in the hoofprints of a legend to claim Grand National glory for the second consecutive year.

Not since Red Rum triumphed at Aintree for the second of three times in 1974 had a horse conquered this most iconic test of equine endeavour more than once.

Through his exploits Red Rum became a household name, his performances on this Liverpool turf as vivid now as all those decades ago. Now, at long last, we have a worthy successor.

Like dear Rummy, Tiger Roll is small in stature but huge in all other regards.

5.15 RACE 6
Randox Health Grand National Handicap Chase (Class 1) (Grade 3)
Winner £500,000
4m2½f (4m2f74y)

Tote Scoop6: Leg 5 **Going: SOFT, Good to Soft in places**

£1,000,000 guaranteed For 7yo+ rated 125 or more. **Highest wt** 11st10lb **Minimum weight** 10st Anibale Fly's Handicap Mark 164 **Entries** 112 pay £1,700 **1st Forfeit** 100 pay £1,700 **2nd Forfeit** 81 pay £1,100 **Confirmed** 69 pay £1,700. **Penalty value 1st** £500,000 **2nd** £200,000 **3rd** £100,000 **4th** £65,000 **5th** £40,000 **6th** £30,000 **7th** £20,000 **8th** £15,000, **9th** £10,000, **10th** £5,000

No	Form	Horse	Jockey	Wt	OR
1	F34-622	ANIBALE FLY (FR) 22 §5 *b g Assessor-Nouba Fly* A J Martin (IRE) John P McManus	t9 11-10 Sean Bowen	11-10	178
22	182-006	MONBEG NOTORIOUS (IRE) 27 §5 *b g Milan-Borleagh Princess* Gordon Elliott (IRE) Gigginstown House Stud	v8 10-10 Sean Bowen	10-10	173
2	32-671P	VALTOR (FR) 70 §6 *b g Nidor-Jossca* Nicky Henderson Simon Munir & Isaac Souede	10 11-6 Daryl Jacob	11-6	169
23	79-5122	RAMSES DE TEILLEE (FR) 49 §3 *gr g Martaline-Princesse d'Orton* David Pipe John White & Anne Underhill	t7 10-9 David Noonan	10-9	177
3	511-411	TIGER ROLL (IRE) 24 §4 C1 *b g Authorized-Swiss Roll* Gordon Elliott (IRE) Gigginstown House Stud	th9 11-5 Davy Russell	11-5	180
24	6-P36PU	TEA FOR TWO 24 §3 *b g Kayf Tara-One For Me* Mrs Jane Williams Mrs Jane Williams & Len Jakeman	10 10-9 Lizzie Kelly	10-9	173
4	8-23544	OUTLANDER (IRE) 42 §6 *b g Stowaway-Western Whisper* Richard Spencer Gowing's Eleven	11 11-4 James Bowen	11-4	173
25	4P100/7	JUST A PAR (IRE) 119 §2 *b g Island House-Thebrownhen* James Moffatt M Scott	b12 10-2 Aidan Coleman	10-2	170
5	P23/PP3	DON POLI (IRE) 21 §6 *b g Poliglote-Dalamine* Philip Kirby Darren & Annaley Yates	p10 11-3 Mr P W Mullins	11-3	174
26	2311-76	STEP BACK (IRE) 84 *ch g Indian River-Steptoutmary* Mark Bradstock Cracker And Smodge Partnership	9 10-7 Nico de Boinville	10-7	174
6	U58-321	GO CONQUER (IRE) 70 §1 *b g Arcadio-Ballinamona Wish* Nigel Twiston-Davies Paul & Clare Rooney	t10 11-3 Sam Twiston-Davies	11-3	174
27	01-435P	ULTRAGOLD (FR) 24 §4 §2 *b/br g Kapgarde-Hot d'Or* Colin Tizzard Brocade Racing J P Romans Terry Warner	t11 10-7 Tom O'Brien	10-7	173
7	1P12-82	MALA BEACH (IRE) 21 BF §6 *b g Beneficial-Peppardstown* Gordon Elliott (IRE) C Jones	11 11-2 Mr J J Codd	11-2	171
28	1273P6P	BLOW BY BLOW (IRE) 27 §6 *ch g Robin Des Champs-Shean Rose* Gordon Elliott (IRE) Gigginstown House Stud	w1 h8 10-6 Andrew Ring	10-6	170
8	P4F-59P	MINELLA ROCCO (IRE) 25 §2 *b g Shirocco-Petralona* Jonjo O'Neill John P McManus	9 11-1 Richie McLernon	11-1	173
29	148-138	UP FOR REVIEW (IRE) 25 BF §4 *ch g Presenting-Coolsilver* W P Mullins (IRE) Andrea & Graham Wylie	10 10-6 Danny Mullins	10-6	170
9	123-113	LAKE VIEW LAD (IRE) 25 §7 *gr g Oscar-Missy O'Brien* N W Alexander Trevor Hemmings	9 11-1 Henry Brooke	11-1	173
30	P52-420	SINGLEFARMPAYMENT 25 §2 *b g Milan-Creavemoy* Tom George N T Griffith & H M Haddock	h9 10-6 Paddy Brennan	10-6	174
10	/0P2-00	PLEASANT COMPANY (IRE) 72 §2 *b g Presenting-Katie Flame* W P Mullins (IRE) Malcolm C Denmark	11 11-1 Paul Townend	11-1	174
31	749-2PP	VIEUX LION ROUGE (FR) 49 §7 C1 *ch g Sabiango-Indecise* David Pipe Prof Caroline Tisdall & John Gent	tp10 10-6 Tom Scudamore	10-6	174
11	142-F6P	BALLYOPTIC (IRE) 49 §5 *b g Old Vic-Lambourne Lace* Nigel Twiston-Davies Mills & Mason Partnership	9 11-1 Tom Bellamy	11-1	171
32	0260930	VALSEUR LIDO (FR) 23 §5 *b g Anzillero-Libido Rock* Henry de Bromhead (IRE) Gigginstown House Stud	10 10-6 Rachael Blackmore	10-6	176
12	PP-07F1	DOUNIKOS (FR) 55 §3 *b g Smadoun-Baby Sitter* Gordon Elliott (IRE) Gigginstown House Stud	11 11-0 Jack Kennedy	11-0	173
33	233-1P2	VINTAGE CLOUDS (IRE) 25 §2 *gr g Cloudings-Rare Vintage* Sue Smith Trevor Hemmings	w2 9 10-6 Danny Cook	10-6	175
13	2BU14-1	RATHVINDEN (IRE) 42 §5 F1 *b g Heron Island-Peggy Cullen* W P Mullins (IRE) R A Bartlett	Hc1 11 11-0 R Walsh	11-0	173
34	1-0953P	GENERAL PRINCIPLE (IRE) 25 §5 *b g Gold Well-How Provincial* Gordon Elliott (IRE) Gigginstown House Stud	t10 10-4 J J Slevin	10-4	173
14	1511/UU	ONE FOR ARTHUR (IRE) 77 §4 C1 *b g Milan-Nonnetia* Lucinda Russell Two Golf Widows	t10 11-0 Derek Fox	11-0	174
35	13F-P20	LIVELOVELAUGH (IRE) 23 §3 *b g Beneficial-Another Evening* W P Mullins (IRE) Mrs S Ricci	8 10-4 David Mullins	10-4	172
15	1P2-616	ROCK THE KASBAH (IRE) 113 §6 *ch g Shirocco-Impudent* Philip Hobbs Mrs Diana L Whateley	p9 10-13 Richard Johnson	10-13	172
36	3P-3133	WALK IN THE MILL (FR) 119 (32H) BF §4 C1 *b g Walk In The Park-Libre Amour* Robert Walford Baroness Harding	9 10-4 James Best	10-4	172
16	2P-41P0	WARRIORS TALE 35 §3 F1 *b g Midnight Legend-Samandara* Paul Nicholls Trevor Hemmings	t10 10-13 Harry Cobden	10-13	171
37	40-4846	FOLSOM BLUE (IRE) 21 BF §7 *b g Old Vic-Spirit Leader* Gordon Elliott (IRE) Core Partnership	tp12 10-4 L P Dempsey	10-4	172
17	3P1P-63	REGAL ENCORE (IRE) 49 §2 *b g King's Theatre-Go On Eileen* Anthony Honeyball John P McManus	11 10-12 Mark Walsh	10-12	170
38	-339613	CAPTAIN REDBEARD (IRE) 35 §3 *ch g Bach-Diesel Dancer* Stuart Coltherd S Coltherd	10 10-3 Sam Coltherd	10-3	172
18	-3112U7	MAGIC OF LIGHT (IRE) 25 §4 *b m Flemensfirth-Quest Of Passion* Mrs John Harrington (IRE) Ann & Alan Potts Limited	p8 10-11 Paddy Kennedy	10-11	173
39	34-566P	BLESS THE WINGS (IRE) 24 §1 *b g Winged Love-Silva Venture* Gordon Elliott (IRE) Adrian Butler/S P O'Connor	p14 10-3 Robert Dunne	10-3	169
19	637P545	A TOI PHIL (FR) 76 (23H) §6 *b g Day Flight-Lucidrile* Gordon Elliott (IRE) Gigginstown House Stud	t9 10-11 Denis O'Regan	10-11	176
40	4311-62	JOE FARRELL (IRE) 14 §7 *b g Presenting-Luck Of The Deise* Rebecca Curtis M Sherwood, N Morris & J Turner	10 10-2 Adam Wedge	10-2	180
20	3-37211	JURY DUTY (IRE) 21 §5 *b g Well Chosen-Swan Heart* Gordon Elliott (IRE) Sideways Syndicate	t8 10-11 Robbie Power	10-11	176
21	4136/90	NOBLE ENDEAVOR (IRE) 25 §4 *b g Flemensfirth-Old Moon* Gordon Elliott (IRE) C Jones	p10 10-10 Mark Enright	10-10	176

2018 (38 ran) Tiger Roll Gordon Elliott 8 10-13 10/1 Davy Russell OR150

POSTDATA Tiger Roll **RP RATING** Tiger Roll

●**FORM PAGE 88** **NEXT RACE** 5.35 Chepstow SKY p63

●**JUST A PAR**, who carries 10-2, is number 25 on the card because it was brought into the race as first reserve following the withdrawal of Mall Dini, the original number 25.

BETTING FORECAST: 4 Tiger Roll, 10 Rathvinden, 12 Vintage Clouds, 14 Anibale Fly, Lake View Lad, 16 Joe Farrell, Jury Duty, Pleasant Company, Rock The Kasbah, 20 Ramses De Teillee, 25 One For Arthur, Step Back, Walk In The Mill, 33 Ballyoptic, Dounikos, General Principle, Noble Endeavor, Up For Review, Vieux Lion Rouge, 50 Captain Redbeard, Livelovelaugh, Mala Beach, Monbeg Notorious, Singlefarmpayment, Tea For Two, Ultragold, Valtor, Warriors Tale, 66 A Toi Phil, Bless The Wings, Don Poli, Magic Of Light, Regal Encore, Valseur Lido, 100 Blow By Blow, Just A Par, Outlander

SPOTLIGHT RICHARD AUSTEN'S VERDICT

Having held off **Pleasant Company** for Aintree glory in 2018, **Tiger Roll** has come roaring back this season and took the latest of his many Cheltenham Festival honours with such ease that he brings improved form to this year's National as well as the 9lb higher mark. The chief negative about him has been the odds in a 40-runner contest. One opponent who could relish his first crack at the race is the Scottish National winner **JOE FARRELL (nap)** who returned to action recently and has shaped very promisingly, as has **Rathvinden** who's another to have registered an important win over 4m last term. **Vintage Clouds** and **Lake View Lad** shaped well with their strong finishes at Cheltenham, while **Step Back** should be primed for a bold show. Although **Tiger Roll** heads the Elliott/Gigginstown horde, **Dounikos (nap)** and **General Principle** could provide them with further powerful ammunition. All will have something to fear if **Minella Rocco** is still in contention after the first circuit.

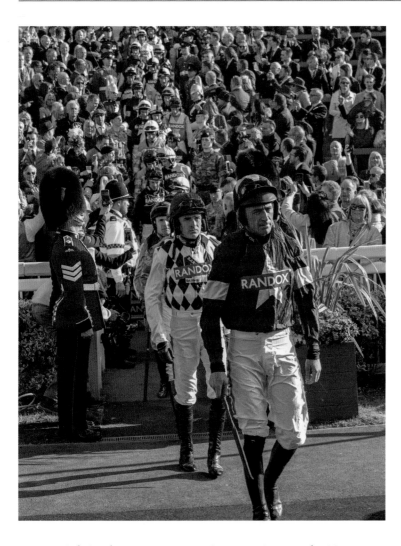

Davy Russell leads the jockeys into the parade ring before the Grand National in April 2019

His relish for this race was every bit as evident as it had been 12 months ago, when he so nearly forfeited a long lead to hold on by a head. This time there was no such drama.

The road to immortality lasted just over four and a quarter miles and ended with Tiger Roll achieving what for so many of his predecessors had been mission impossible. Under a blue sky, and with the world watching, he sprinted to superstardom under a magnificent Davy Russell, two and three-quarter lengths clear of Magic Of Light, the only mare in the 40-runner field.

Scenes of euphoria broke out all around this most special part of Merseyside as 70,000 people realised they had been present for a special moment. Among that happy throng there were none more

Following spread: Davy Russell stands tall in the saddle after a second Grand National triumph on Tiger Roll

Davy Russell goes down to kiss his more-than-
willing partner

ecstatic than Tiger Roll's adoring trainer Gordon Elliott, who looked
close to spontaneously combusting with joy from the second he was
reunited with the horse who has changed his life.

'He's the horse of a lifetime,' said Elliott, while equally in thrall
to a thoroughbred he once branded 'a little rat' was Gigginstown
House Stud's Michael O'Leary, the Ryanair magnate who built a
budget airline and now owns a horse money couldn't buy. That
horse, he announced, will not seek to emulate Red Rum by winning
a third National. He will surely reserve the right to change his mind.

'To win two Grand Nationals is unbelievable,' said O'Leary. 'He's
a legend. He's now in that bracket with Red Rum. It's incredible.'

Nobody would dispute those handsome words but this was not
a perfect day, for at the opening fence a fatal injury was suffered by
Up For Review, the first horse to be lost in the Grand National since
2012.

That fence then had to be bypassed on the second circuit,
meaning what at that point was still a 37-strong field had to
negotiate a tight chicane. That task was completed brilliantly by

the jockeys, none of whom were sitting as happily as Russell. His happiness was not about to fade.

For in a contest in which only seven horses parted company with their riders, Tiger Roll, a quadruple Cheltenham Festival champion, travelled with ominous ease throughout. He was running off a 9lb higher mark than last year and had 11st 5lb on his back, but he skipped over the green spruce fences, low and clean, save for a couple of hairy leaps on the final run back to the racecourse proper.

Yet there is surely no horse in training who knows more about his job than the nine-year-old, who was still cruising alongside Magic Of Light at the last. She got that badly wrong. Tiger Roll got it gloriously right and powered clear, with Rathvinden third and Walk In The Mill fourth.

As the 4-1 favourite, Tiger Roll was the shortest-priced winner in 100 years. Just another reason for us to worship him.

'Everyone loves him,' said Elliott, who had been responsible for an unprecedented 11 runners but rewrote the record books in an even better way.

'He's a little like myself,' he added. 'He likes the good life. He eats, sleeps and drinks. And he wants to win. He's the people's horse.'

That people's horse won the people's race, as Russell so rightly observed.

'This horse and this place are amazing,' he said. 'Liverpool and Aintree are so far ahead. They should be proud of what they have here. I'm proud to be part of it.'

He then turned his pride towards Tiger Roll.

'This horse is unreal,' said Russell. 'He actually knows his name. When the commentator said his name as we were parading he perked up. He's so intelligent it's unbelievable.'

The 39-year-old Russell now has two National wins to his own name. Elliott and O'Leary, who struck independently with Silver Birch and Rule The World, have three. Whether Tiger Roll will get the chance to turn two into three and mirror Red Rum is, at this point, far from certain.

'It's unlikely he'll come back next year,' said O'Leary. 'His main goal is the Cross Country Chase. If he wins that a third time we'll retire him. In business you can be greedy. In racing you shouldn't be greedy.'

Crucially, O'Leary did offer a welcome glimmer of hope. 'We'll work out next year, next year,' he said, adding: 'Let's just enjoy this day.'

It was a day we shall never forget. For this was the day when Tiger Roll joined the immortals.

AINTREE

April 6, 2019

Randox Health Grand National Handicap
Chase
4m2½f

1	Tiger Roll	Davy Russell	4-1f
2	Magic Of Light	Paddy Kennedy	66-1
3	Rathvinden	Ruby Walsh	8-1

2¾ lengths, 2¼ lengths
40 ran

RACING POST ANALYSIS – Dave Orton

This was a classy Grand National and there was no let-up from the first fence. It saw the dream result with Tiger Roll becoming the first horse to successfully defend the title since the mighty Red Rum in the 1970s. The form is outstanding.

Tiger Roll got an outstanding ride from Davy Russell and followed up last year's success in ready fashion. He had a 9lb higher mark this time around, but was actually 8lb ahead of the handicapper courtesy of his romp in the Cross Country at last month's Cheltenham Festival.

Russell tracked main market rival Rathvinden on the first circuit and one could tell six out he was confident. He did well to recover from a bad mistake four from home and once the runner-up hit the last went into a clear lead. As was the case last year, he seemed to idle up the run-in and it's hard to gauge how much he had up his sleeve at the finish.

Next season it will be a surprise if he's not carrying top weight, but it has to be remembered he's still just a nine-year-old and might not have reached his peak just yet. It will take a seriously well-handicapped rival to stop him from becoming the first horse to win the race three times in a row in 2020. He's very special.

After the race Stuart Riley spoke to Donald McCain, among others, at Aintree for their reaction:

'It takes a special horse to do it round here'

DONALD McCAIN

Donald McCain knows what it takes to win a Grand National. His father, Ginger, is the joint most successful trainer in the history of the race having been responsible for three-time winner Red Rum, so his son is as well placed as anyone to evaluate what everyone at Aintree witnessed on Saturday and labelled it 'a very special performance'.

McCain had said in the build-up the demands of the race had changed and the task Tiger Roll faced off a 9lb higher mark was not as stiff as that Red Rum overcame in 1973, 1974 and 1977. But no one loves this place as much as McCain and he was as blown away as anyone.

'That's a very special performance,' he said. 'Full credit to Gordon Elliott, he's made a great job of him. He was never going to get beat from four out, was he?

'It takes a very special horse to do it round here, and in a way they've come a similar route as a failed Flat horse. It's taken an awful long time for someone to do it [go back-to-back like Red Rum], let's see if they can do it again next year.'

Leading owner JP McManus was in agreement and said: 'It's great for the game. He's a great winner – and deserved to win. He had it won from a mile out.'

Jonjo O'Neill, who never won the race as a jockey but saddled Don't Push It to win for McManus in 2010, added: 'He's a machine, great to watch and good for the game.'

BHA chief handicapper Martin Greenwood was impressed and suggested it could go down as the greatest performance in the history of the great race.

'That was amazing,' he said. 'It was possibly the best Grand National of all time. He's going to be rated in the low-170s. He was only pushed out towards the end, he tanked along for most of the race, he was still on the bridle at the Elbow. He's going to be Gold Cup-standard.'

Jessica Harrington, trainer of runner-up Magic Of Light, said: 'Tiger Roll is an amazing horse, and much better this year than last. He's the most gorgeous little horse, a joy to watch over these fences.'

Ted Walsh, who saddled Papillon to win the race in 2000, added: 'He's a magic horse. A unique little horse, very like Red Rum, who was bred for the Flat. He got a great ride and it was a great training performance. He's everything the National is about.'

David Baxter looked back to where Tiger Roll started his career:

It could have all been so different. A cursory glance at Tiger Roll's pedigree reveals a horse who should have become a middle-distance type on the Flat, not a dual Grand National winner.

A son of Authorized, Tiger Roll was first purchased for 70,000gns as a foal in November 2010 by John Ferguson on behalf of Godolphin.

The anticipated Flat career failed to catch on, so nearly three years later Tiger Roll was back at the sales, this time fetching a more modest £10,000 and joining Nigel Hawke in Devon.

'I like buying from Godolphin as there are a lot of well-bred, nice horses who come from that area and they can be a little bit big and backward or a little bit slow,' Hawke said yesterday.

'Tiger Roll ticked all the boxes. He was well bred and correct. He wasn't the biggest in the world but the plan was to buy him,

'He's a great winner – and deserved to win'

JP McMANUS

'He's the most gorgeous little horse'

JESSICA HARRINGTON

bring him along to run well in a mile-and-a-half bumper and sell him on.'

However, that plan was tinkered with when Tiger Roll was presented with hurdles. Market Rasen on Sunday November 10, 2013, was the starting point for the then three-year-old's career and there were embryonic signs of his nimble jumping ability and powerful engine as the 12-1 chance won by three and three-quarter lengths.

Hawke added: 'We went straight to a juvenile hurdle because his jumping was so good. It's rare a horse wins a juvenile first time out having never been on track before but he was capable of doing it. He was a natural jumper.'

With that successful outing in the books, Tiger Roll found himself back under the auctioneer's hammer the following month, when Mags O'Toole was the purchaser of lot nine at the Brightwells Cheltenham sale for £80,000. He joined Gordon Elliott and the rest, as they say, is history.

Hawke does not stay awake long into the night wondering what could have been. He takes the opposite view, and was cheering him on at home on Saturday.

'I thought he was tailor-made for the Fred Winter,' Hawke said. 'They went the Triumph route but he was a perfect four-year-old hurdler. You'd never visualise three or four years down the line he'd achieve what he has. He's got racing in his comfort zone and has never stopped improving.

'It's just a pleasure to think I was a small cog in all of it. It's an incredible story and the horse is an absolute dream.'

Although he missed out on the ride because he was unable to do the weight at Aintree, Keith Donoghue was as proud as anyone associated with Tiger Roll as David Jennings found out:

Incredibly clever is how Keith Donoghue has described Tiger Roll after he emulated Red Rum by defending his Grand National crown on Saturday, and the rider is already licking his lips at the prospect of partnering racing's latest legend in next year's Cross Country Chase at the Cheltenham Festival.

Donoghue knows Tiger Roll better than most having been on board for six of his last eight starts and he watched his buddy create history under Davy Russell from the comfort of the Aintree grandstand on Saturday.

His intended National mount Outlander was sold on Thursday night, with new connections booking James Bowen.

'Once I wasn't riding for Gordon [Elliott] with Outlander running under a different trainer, it didn't bother me too much,' he reflected on Sunday.

'I'd have loved to have ridden in the race, but I wasn't devastated. It meant more to me that I was riding for Gordon. He's been the one who has saved my career.'

Unlike last year's Grand National, when Donoghue finished eighth on Valseur Lido, this time he was able to watch Tiger Roll's every move alongside his father Michael, and he knew history was in the making from a very early stage.

Donoghue said: 'He was loving it from the word go and always looked happy. He always just finds positions for himself. He makes things so easy for whoever's on him.

'He's incredibly clever. When I won the Boyne Hurdle on him at Navan, he clipped the top bar of every hurdle. If I hadn't known him I'd have told Gordon there's no way he could ever run in a chase. But that's just him.

'Whether he's jumping a hurdle or jumping the Chair he knows exactly how much height he needs to clear it. It doesn't matter to him what he's jumping.'

Donoghue is already gazing into the future and imagining what it will be like to ride Tiger Roll in his hat-trick attempt in the Cross Country Chase at Cheltenham in 2020.

'He'll be the shortest price in Cheltenham history, won't he?' said Donoghue.

'What a little legend he is. The thing about him now is that he knows how good he is. He absolutely adores the attention. The more confident he is, the better he is. He knows he's top dog.

'Getting to ride him around Navan was a bonus for me this year. I was delighted to see him winning the National again as much as anybody. I'd have loved to ride him but certainly didn't begrudge Davy winning on him again. I had my day in the sun at Cheltenham and hopefully will get another day like that next year.'

David Jennings was also on hand for Tiger Roll's homecoming in County Meath the day after the Grand National:

We have been here before, haven't we? Same street, same village, same occasion, same horse. An overwhelming sense of déjà vu should have smothered Summerhill, the small village in County Meath where Gordon Elliott grew up. Yet this wasn't the same at all. This was a proper shindig.

Previous spread: Tiger Roll is surrounded by a sea of people as he walks through Summerhill the day after his second Grand National victory

Hundreds turned into thousands, cheers turned into chants and Tiger Roll turned into a legend never to be forgotten in racing folklore. It's smaller he is getting, you know.

'He's not very big, Mammy, is he? George is almost as big as him,' says four-year-old Matt Smyth, sitting on his mother's shoulders as Tiger Roll disembarks the horse box to a chorus of cheers at the end of the street. George, I find out later, is the Smyth family's golden retriever.

The 'little rat', as owner Michael O'Leary described him before he became an A-list celebrity, has turned into the most precious little horse in racing, on Saturday becoming the first since Red Rum in the 1970s to win back-to-back Grand Nationals.

'I never thought we'd win a Grand National in my lifetime, never mind three of them in four years, it's phenomenal,' says O'Leary, the Gigginstown House Stud supremo who won the 2016 National with Rule The World and is now far more complimentary about Tiger Roll.

Tiger Roll in front of his adoring fans in Summerhill

'People are comparing him to Red Rum,' he continues. 'That's unbelievable for him to be mentioned in the same sentence as Red

Rum. The atmosphere at Aintree was electric yesterday. There was a lot of expectation he'd win again and he was hot favourite, but very rarely does the hot favourite win the Grand National.'

They do now, which is why O'Leary, who is also boss of Ryanair, doubled his offer from last year to give those on the flight back to Ireland from Liverpool on Saturday evening two free drinks, and it's why thousands turned up to see his history-making horse.

'The horse is now officially a superstar,' says Michael's brother Eddie. 'I wasn't here last year but the turnout is amazing, I can't believe it. He deserves every single cheer he's getting.

'When he went to the front at the Elbow, I just closed my eyes. I couldn't watch. For this horse to do the un-doable was unbelievable.'

As Elliott poses for selfie after selfie – he's perfected the selfie smile, by the way – his assistant Aidan O'Ryan explains the emotion the pair went through watching the closing stages together in the middle of the track.

'Gordon was actually very calm during the race,' relays O'Ryan. 'We had 11 in the race so we were trying to find them all at various

Top: Gordon Elliott and Michael O'Leary with Tiger Roll

Bottom: Tiger Roll with Davy Russell

Louise Dunne with Tiger Roll – her pride and joy

stages. It was a case of, "There's another one gone, and another one."

'From four out Dounikos was the only other one involved, then he made a bad mistake and dropped out, so it was a case of Tiger Roll or nothing.

'Madness. That's the only word I can use to describe what it was like from the last to the line. There was a heap of us there and we all jumped on each other. Myself, Jack Madden and Gordon made an absolute show of ourselves. It was a great release of emotion.'

There are plenty of emotions being released on the streets of Summerhill too as Michael O'Leary calls for three cheers for Elliott. He could have asked for 33 and the crowd would have obliged. They are terribly proud of him around these parts.

Let's hear from a chap who went to school with Elliott.

'I was in the same class as Gordon – we went to St Michael's in Trim,' says John Donoghue, a native of Killeen, a few miles down the road.

'I was here after Don Cossack won the Gold Cup and was in Dunshaughlin after Klairon Davis did the business in the Champion Chase, but nothing compares to this. I've never seen crowds like this welcoming home a horse.'

The selfies are slowing down so it seems the perfect time to grab Elliott.

'It's only still just sinking in,' he admits. 'I'm a proud Summerhill man. It's a great community here and I see a lot of familiar faces lining the streets, so to win the biggest race in the world with the same horse again is very special.'

Michael O'Leary feels a third Cross Country Chase win at Cheltenham in March would be the perfect swansong for Tiger Roll, but does the trainer think we'll be back in 12 months for a third National homecoming parade?

'Who knows, maybe,' he replies. 'This horse can do anything. We'll get this year's celebrations out of the way first, though. We're going to enjoy tonight.'

And what does tonight consist of?

'Just a few quiet drinks in Shaw's, but I'm not going home until you buy me a pint, David,' comes the answer.

Elliott is still in Shaw's. If you're reading this, the ATM was out of order.

Alastair Down reflected on a day when a nation put its differences aside in awe of a special diminutive hero:

On an indelible Aintree Saturday the angels gave us more than a mere glimpse of the sunlit uplands when Tiger Roll scampered all but seamlessly to a second Grand National victory that left the 70,000 on hand reeling with the feeling that it was, indeed, magnificent to be alive.

Across a nation close to exhausted by schism and division we suddenly had bestowed upon us a moment of utter unity – all brought about by a diminutive thoroughbred endowed with a heart the size of a continent.

And after a Cheltenham Festival that sowed an absurd amount of discord, here was the affirming, pulsating and tear-duct-flushing afternoon jump racing needed.

Cometh the hour, cometh the horse. It is an enduring matter of wonder the places they can take us. The heights horses reach that no early Himalayan pioneer – tweed-clad and armed with no more than a brace of Sherpas – could contemplate conquering.

If you want to understand tigers there is only one man to go to – Jim Corbett (1875-1955) who was a bachelor colonial official born in India and after whom that nation's first national park for the preservation of the striped majesties was named.

That honour tells you all you need to know about the reverence in which his knowledge was held.

His fame rests on killing man-eaters such as the Champawat tiger, who is documented as killing 436 of we lesser creatures. But Corbett, jungle-wise like few others, was as skilled with a camera as a rifle and was a passionate advocate of the tiger.

Tiger Roll (blinkers right) safely negotiates
Becher's Brook on the first circuit

In the early 20th century Jim was a groundbreaking conservationist when the word meant somebody who made jam.

Fittingly, his words rattle down the years to describe that which we witnessed at Aintree: 'There are events in one's life which, however remote, never fade from memory.'

Spot on, sir, because this was the sort of moment in which shivered timbers are shaped.

To my eye Tiger Roll had it won after they had jumped about ten. Yes, there were a couple of fluffed fences second time around but the palpable pecks were little more than you see from a sparrow nicking a seed from a bird table.

He is not a horse who gets high at his fences but he is canny like a fox. No high-wire walker over Niagara ever had his balance or poise.

When he gets in close it is almost as if he is saying: 'Hey, Russell, you are getting paid for this gig so just bloody concentrate. I'm the one doing the graft here.'

From four fences out it was a question of 'referee stop the contest'. And of course all of us watching sensed the moment and started the salutation of acclamation. Across the islands, in front of countless televisions, the celebrations will have begun by then – tigers roar but in millions of homes the primeval sound will have been echoed in ferocity as we willed him on to immortality.

People always want to know where a horse stands in the pantheon. Well we are not talking Arkles or Kauto Stars here. Perhaps we are talking about something more important. Forget that dry old term esteem and unleash the L-word. We love him.

In my decades pretending to work, the horses most loved by the rank and file of the faithful have been Red Rum and Desert Orchid, but the two are now three.

At this level of joy comparisons are as iniquitous as they are fatuous. Red Rum won three Nationals and was twice second, Desert Orchid illuminated winter afternoons more brightly than the beacons that signalled the sighting of the Spanish Armada, yet here is a cherub – though no angel – who has won two of the acid Aintree tests plus a scarcely credible four festival races.

Such horses are the Fabergé eggs of jump racing – objects of incalculable beauty, incredibly rare and beyond price.

I am privileged to have a little bit of history with Tiger Roll. On December 13, 2013, I happened to be standing next to legendary buyer Mags O'Toole at a Cheltenham sale when she bought him for 80 grand – a little ferret of a thing who might be good enough to run in the Triumph Hurdle. Mags and Eddie O'Leary also bought some other yoke for north of £200,000 that dusk.

Late in the evening around eight of us gathered in an architecturally spectacular Cheltenham restaurant converted from a redundant church – think red wine and pizza rather than communion wafers.

It was all going along nicely until Eddie O'Leary – and if you think Michael is bonkers you should meet the brother – let Gordon Elliott know he was getting Tiger Roll rather than the absurdly expensive one.

Tiger Roll clears the final fence with a slight advantage over Magic Of Light

Davy Russell throws a bucket of water over
Tiger Roll after the race

To say Elliott was displeased at the news is something of an understatement.

Elliott is an extraordinary figure whom it took years for me to fathom. When he won the National with the Paul Nicholls retread Silver Birch, he sat in the press conference with the air of a man who did not know if it was Pancake Tuesday or Halloween.

He simply had no grasp of what he had achieved. So-called clever folk – hands up here – thought it some sort of a fluke. How absurdly wrong can one be? But the O'Leary brothers saw something the rest of the world let glide over their heads. Eddie and Michael are not merely tough – they can be hard and the only passengers they tolerate pay for early boarding.

But Elliott is a phenomenon, an outsider whose dad was a panel beater. And where did he learn? At Martin Pipe's, another outsider whose dad was a bookie.

They say Elliott is frightened of nobody except Carol Pipe – a benevolent dictatress if there ever was one.

Two pre-National memories lodge in the mind.

Before racing on Saturday there was time for a swift pint with Eddie and Gordon. Michael was barred because he had not been in the same bar the year before so it would have been bad luck to have him there.

And then down at the start Tiger Roll was plenty wound up and Greta Garbo-ing it off on his own. Denis O'Regan, sensing the moment, brought the Elliott 20th string A Toi Phil over to nurture and usher him back to the main group of runners.

A small stroke of genius that chilled the favourite away from getting more fretful. Of such tiny actions great events are fettled.

After the race Michael O'Leary was full of the idea Tiger Roll would not return for the great race next year. Just as he was full of tosh post-Cheltenham that the little warrior would not go to Aintree.

I am sorry Michael but it is out of your hands. Few geniuses – and you are one – have a finer line in producing words which rhyme with rollocks, but the choice is no longer yours.

Yes his rampant Gurkha would have to carry 5lb more. Would it bother him? Not a scrap.

Tiger Roll has passed out of your hands into the hearts of all those who love an indomitable and adorable racehorse.

See you all next year. Not to beat records but to keep all our hearts thumping. As they did on Saturday's imperishable afternoon.

Martin Stevens spoke again to Jerry O'Brien, who was at Aintree to cheer on his homebred son of Authorized:

A face in the crowds as Tiger Roll was welcomed into the Aintree winner's enclosure after the horse's historic second Grand National victory on Saturday was his modest yet charismatic breeder Jerry O'Brien.

The former member of Coolmore's veterinary staff had made the journey from his farm near Portroe, County Tipperary – home of Tiger Roll's dam Swiss Roll – to London for the weekend, with a train trip to Liverpool bookended by a visit to some of the capital's galleries.

The work of art closest to O'Brien's heart, though, is the four-time Cheltenham Festival winner and now dual National hero whom he bred by sending his Entrepreneur mare Swiss Roll to Derby victor Authorized.

'I got to Aintree in the morning and walked the first three fences and then the chairman of the course and the sponsors asked me to a reception before the race, so I had a few drinks and then made my way to the parade ring for the race,' he said.

'It was a great race, he was going so well, but then he made those three mistakes coming up the straight, one, two, three, and I thought he was gone. It was great horsemanship from Davy Russell that he stayed upright.'

One memory from the day in particular brought home for O'Brien how Tiger Roll has become an icon of the sport.

He said: 'There was a lady standing beside me with a kid in a pushchair as we waited for the horses to come back in, and he was saying 'Mummy, Mummy, when is the Tiger coming?'

'The horse has captured the imagination and given so much pleasure to everyone – it's great for racing.'

O'Brien, recipient of the National Hunt achievement prize at the ITBA awards in January, has been responding to phone calls from friends and messages of congratulations from well-wishers since his return to Tipperary.

As for the 19-year-old Swiss Roll, she is due to give birth to a Teofilo foal who will be a full sibling to the progressive stayer Austrian School in a couple of weeks.

Davy Russell holds on tight to the trophy after the Grand National

The mare has a yearling filly by Exceed And Excel who is likely to be heading for the sales this autumn – which one depends on the advice of Bill Dwan, who prepared Tiger Roll to be sold as a foal and is dubbed 'The Guru' by O'Brien – while she also has a two-year-old colt by Teofilo.

O'Brien spoke more about his day at Aintree and what the Grand National – and Tiger Roll – meant to him:

Sometimes less is more, and words can't describe the virtuosity and artistry displayed by Davy Russell on board Aintree's hero, Tiger Roll, amplified and embellished by the brilliance of trainer Gordon Elliott and his team. You have to see it to believe it.

I'd like to thank Rose Paterson, chairman of Aintree, and the sponsors Randox for inviting me to a most enjoyable reception. It was my first time at the Grand National and what a day to remember; unlike true love, it will last forever.

My grandfather in the auld days used to attend the Grand National every year as a spectator, as he was over and back from Ireland to Birkenhead shipping cattle on a weekly basis.

His son, my father – like me, an only child – never got the chance to follow his father. He ended up in Smithfield Market in London trading meat for 20 years until finally he came home to my mother and me to open a butcher's stall. We had very happy and wonderful times together, and my success with Tiger Roll is for them.

Is there more to come from the Tiger? Is the glass still only half full? Only time will tell. As for him being that 'little rat of a thing, not a good horse, not a class horse, just a complete overachiever', suffice to say let sleeping dogs lie!

The official handicapper then had his take on Tiger Roll's Grand National victory as Bruce Jackson reported:

Tiger Roll's historic second Grand National success has been ranked the best performance in the race for 46 years, eclipsing the legendary Red Rum whose feat of back-to-back victories he so memorably emulated on Saturday.

BHA handicapper Martin Greenwood said on Tuesday that a rating of 172 given to Tiger Roll has been surpassed only by Crisp, the gallant runner-up off top weight to Red Rum in 1973, since meaningful records began in the same year.

Greenwood, who also stated the performance was good enough for Tiger Roll to have finished second in last month's Cheltenham Gold Cup, wrote on his BHA handicapper's blog: 'I am suggesting that Tiger Roll has put up the best winning performance in any National from 1973 to present, beating Many Clouds (167) in 2015 and Neptune Collonges (168) in 2012.

'It also trumps Suny Bay's second (beaten 11 lengths by Earth Summit, conceding him 23lb) off 170 in 1998. Using a Timeform-based assessment of the 1970s it would suggest Red Rum was never higher than 166 with L'Escargot 161 when winning his National, while Crisp was rated 173 when a gallant second in 1973.'

Greenwood added: 'The mighty Tiger is now [rated] 172, which only allows 2lb for the style of his victory given his bare form suggests 170. This figure would have him second in this season's Gold Cup and Betway Bowl.'

Greenwood went on to say he had consulted his predecessor Phil Smith, who framed the weights for the race 20 times before retiring last year, and former Timeform colleagues.

Only Gold Cup winner Al Boum Photo and Aintree Bowl winner Kemboy, who was credited with putting up the same 176-rated performance as Cue Card three years previously in the race, have higher current ratings.

But Greenwood suggests that both Willie Mullins-trained chasers would be put under pressure by Tiger Roll were they ever to meet.

Greenwood added: 'I think 172 could still underestimate him and ever since he reappeared in the Boyne Hurdle at Navan in February – a clear personal best in that discipline – Tiger Roll has looked a different horse, which is remarkable given he has been on the go since 2013 and is great testament to his trainer.'

Peter Thomas compared and contrasted two famous Grand National campaigns:

When Red Rum won his third Grand National in 1977 there were many commentators happy to trot out the line that the great horse's feats were of such magnitude they would never be equalled.

As the decades passed and successive National heroes failed even to back up a lone win in the Aintree showpiece, the myth gained traction – if not carved in stone, then at least inked into racing folklore.

Last Saturday, while Tiger Roll wasn't quite registering his third success in the world's favourite steeplechase, he at least proved winning a second was no longer an impossibility.

Moreover, Tiger Roll has age on his side should he be allowed to attempt a third victory. While Red Rum was a dignified 12 years old when completing his hat-trick, the 2019 hero will be a mere babe in arms at ten and, although he would no doubt be asked to carry top weight of 11st 10lb, Ginger McCain's warrior lumped 12st as a nine-year-old and a not inconsiderable 11st 8lb on his final day of glory.

That, however, is a matter for the future orchestrated by Tiger Roll's impish owner Michael O'Leary.

All we can do now is to compare and contrast the two Aintree greats at the same stage of their respective careers, as they were prepared for their second National successes, although in honesty we may have to contrast far more than we compare.

It's no secret that jump racing, along with just about everything else, has changed a lot between 1974 and 2019. Mostly things have changed for the worse, of course.

Mick Channon, mercifully, is still with us in his incarnation as a trainer, providing a slightly rickety bridge between the two eras, but Marc Bolan has gone and Bruno Mars hasn't; Harold Wilson isn't in power but Donald Trump is; and you can't find a decent pair of loon pants for love nor money.

Whether jump racing has changed for better or for worse is for the reader to decide, but the Grand National preparations of Red Rum and Tiger Roll at least confirm the upheaval that has transpired in the last 45 years and hold a mirror up to wider society.

If Red Rum were in his pomp today, he would be a relic, an old-fashioned centre forward waiting frustratedly for a cross from an extinct old-fashioned winger.

He wasn't very big, and his feet gave him a lot of gyp, but he'd have played 90 minutes every game, all season, elbows flying. He started out as a moderate sprinter and even won a few on the Flat, but he relished the guts and glory of the staying chase division.

Tiger Roll, meanwhile – another teeny, Irish-bred former Flat racer, bought as a Fred Winter type but won a Triumph before being quickly reinvented – has been hailed as the toughest thing since old boots, yet setting his latest campaign against the efforts of his illustrious predecessor is like comparing a stroll in the park to a commando boot camp.

Let's consider what Gordon Elliott demanded of the diminutive son of Authorized. There could certainly have been no sour taste in the mouth of the horse whose mother was called Swiss Roll.

From the moment he won the 2018 National, it was made clear he would be asked to go back to his old stamping ground of

BEST GRAND NATIONAL PERFORMANCES BY OFFICIAL RATING

Crisp	173
Tiger Roll	172
Suny Bay	170
Neptune Collonges	168
Many Clouds	167
Red Rum	166

RED RUM v TIGER ROLL
1974 AND 2019 COMPARED

POLITICALLY
1974 Three-day week
2019 Brexit

NO.1 IN THE MUSIC CHARTS
1974 Paper Lace, Billy Don't Be A Hero
2019 Lewis Capaldi, Someone You Loved

SPORT
1974 Leeds United top the First Division from Liverpool despite losing 3-1 to West Ham on Grand National day
2019 Liverpool lead the Premier League from Manchester City

LIFESTYLE
1974 Average cost of: a pint of lager 20p 20 cigarettes 20p
2019 Average cost of: a pint of lager £3.60 20 cigarettes £12

NATIONAL DAY ATTENDANCE
1974 8,000
2019 70,000

FOOTBALL
1974 Mick Channon is top scorer in the First Division on 21 goals
2019 Sergio Agüero leads the Premier League top scorers with 19 goals

TELEVISION
1974 Jon Pertwee hands over Dr Who role to Tom Baker, the fourth Dr
2019 Jodie Whittaker is the 13th Dr

CHAMPION JOCKEY
1974 Ron Barry is champion jump jockey with **94 wins**
2019 Richard Johnson leads the table with **192 wins**

BOX OFFICE
1974 *Blazing Saddles*
2019 *Captain Marvel*

Red Rum		Tiger Roll
11-1	Starting price	4-1f
9	Age	9
12st	Weight	11st 5lb
7 lengths	Win distance	2¾ lengths
42	Runners	40
9min 20.3sec (distance 4m4f)	Time	9min 1sec (distance 4m2½f)
Good	Going	Good to soft

Cheltenham in November for a jaunt over the cheese wedges and bullfinches before returning for another cross-country caper in March.

The only imponderable lay between the two, and the choice of a 2m5f hurdle at Navan – albeit at Grade 2 level – would hardly have struck fear into the gutsy little fellow's heart.

The first Cheltenham visit ended in a satisfactory fourth place, the hurdle in an unexpected 25-1 win, the festival outing in impressive victory ... and that was it. A few weeks of fine-tuning and it was back to Liverpool for the main event.

Red Rum, meanwhile, was campaigned rather more vigorously. Cotton wool didn't seem to have been invented in 1973, or at least wasn't available in the shops of Southport, where McCain, sheepskin coat and all, galloped his national treasure on the beach and kept him in a box behind his used-car showroom.

It was an environment in which value for money counted for a lot, and Rummy certainly paid his way. Ten runs was the final count in 1973-74, with six wins, one disqualification, a short-head second in the Hennessy and not a cheese wedge or a hurdle in sight.

It was a season that might be described as astonishing were it to be repeated today, although the chances of that are slim. That it worked, that it culminated in victory at Aintree, and then culminated again in victory at Ayr, in no less a test than the Scottish Grand National, is testament either to meticulous planning or to the merits of a horse in a million.

For ever-present rider Brian Fletcher it must have been a joy to partner his old Aintree ally from September 26 – when they 'won' a Perth handicap chase under 12st 4lb, only to be demoted for interference – to April 20, when they landed the big Ayr prize by four lengths from Proud Tarquin.

For most trainers, one National would have been enough, but Red Rum had a deep well of brilliance and resilience and McCain seemed ever to be looking for the bottom of it.

Yes, his pride and joy had been turned out to win three on the trot after Perth – at Carlisle, Ayr and Newcastle – and had then faced a match with his great rival Crisp (famously defeated in the 1973 running in Liverpool), but that was his job.

He may have been asked to give a stone to winner Red Candle when pipped in the Hennessy (viewed by some form book aficionados as his finest hour); he may have scored at Catterick in February under 12st 7lb, but he unseated his rider after the first on his final National prep in the Greenall Whitley at Haydock, so he'd had it easy – sort of.

Aintree was his favourite track, after all, and he was a professional athlete with a zest for life and a will to win, so perhaps he'd had the perfect preparation. It's just that it wasn't Tiger Roll's preparation. The past is, indeed, another country, and Ginger McCain did things very differently there.

Perhaps the two horses aren't so different: two tough nuts defying expectations and embracing the Grand National as the pinnacle of jump racing achievement. But there's one big difference in the way they were managed: as soon as Red Rum passed the post at Aintree in 1974, his owner, Noel Le Mare, and his trainer would have been casting their minds 12 months ahead to a tilt at true racing greatness, with no equivocation. He went back twice more before finally bagging his third National at the fifth attempt.

Ginger would no doubt have been horrified to hear O'Leary say, in jest or otherwise, that Tiger Roll probably won't go back to Liverpool in 2020. After all, what's a National horse for if not to win Nationals?

Tiger Roll's popularity with the racing public was again evident when he was crowned the 2018-19 Racing Post Jumps Horse of the Year.

Having also earned the prize the previous year, Tiger Roll received more than half the votes cast by Racing Post *readers as he galloped to a runaway victory from his four rivals.*

In the middle of May Gigginstown dropped a bombshell on the racing world when they announced their plans to wind down one of the sport's most successful ownership entities over the coming years. The scaling back policy began immediately as the stud did not restock at the stores sales.

Speaking on behalf of his brother Michael O'Leary, Eddie O'Leary said: 'Michael's children are now growing with their activities, leaving less and less time for racing last season and for the foreseeable future.

'We've just had our best season ever in terms of winners and it's been an amazing year capped by Tiger Roll winning the Grand National for the second time last month.

'We have lots of young stock to be allocated among our trainers over the coming weeks and each of our trainers will receive their usual allocation of young point-to-pointers.'

In August Eddie O'Leary outlined what needed to happen for Tiger Roll to go for a Grand National hat-trick as Brian Sheerin reported:

Tiger Roll will aim to emulate the legendary Red Rum by bidding for a third Grand National only if the handicapper allots him a rating of 165 or lower, according to Gigginstown racing manager Eddie O'Leary.

Outlining plans for the dual Grand National hero, O'Leary said: 'He won't run at the Cheltenham November meeting this year because it's a handicap.

'He'll have a run over hurdles before Christmas, then on to the Boyne Hurdle before running in the Cross Country Chase at Cheltenham. If they compress the weights for the Grand National, we'll run – but only if they condense the weights.

'We're rated 172 – if he's off 165 he'll run but if he's off 166 he won't be running.'

O'Leary admitted he had been caught off guard by the outpouring of affection directed towards Tiger Roll – who won last season's race off a mark of 159 – but insists Gordon Elliott and Keith Donoghue deserve all the credit for such heroics.

He added: 'This horse keeps on rewriting the book. Don Cossack was a brilliant horse but Tiger Roll is doing things that no horse has done before. It's a testament to his trainer and all the lads up in Cullentra.

'People forget that this horse had stopped racing. He'd given up the ghost and stopped racing but Gordon and Keith got him back and he's a superstar now. It's incredible. Even we [Eddie and Michael O'Leary] are coming around to the idea that he's a superstar.'

The handicapper responded immediately as David Carr reported:

There will be no special treatment from the handicapper to tempt connections of Tiger Roll to aim for a third Grand National and emulate the legendary Red Rum.

Owner Michael O'Leary has warned Tiger Roll is far from certain to bid for an Aintree hat-trick next April as he does not want to overface him, and racing manager Eddie O'Leary said last week: 'If he's off 165 he'll run, but if he's off 166 he won't be running.'

However, BHA chase handicapper Martin Greenwood, who has the discretion to set his own weights in the National rather than relying on official ratings, has suggested Tiger Roll will be allotted a higher rating than the one sought by connections.

'As always, I'll treat every horse as I see fit when the entries are made in January,' he said. 'They want him 165 or under, he's currently rated 172 and an awful lot of things are going to have to alter markedly for those to converge.

'He won off 159 last year in really good style. He'd been due to go up to 167 at the time; the third and fifth were also both due to go up 8lb, so it was good form. It was one of the best performances in the National in modern times.'

Eddie O'Leary argued for the handicap to be compressed, a practice introduced by Greenwood's predecessor Phil Smith, in order to allow Tiger Roll to run.

Greenwood said: 'Last year I dropped Bristol De Mai to keep horses in the handicap at the bottom, but where Tiger Roll is different is that he runs in handicaps and he has the Aintree factor – he's won the National twice, which means that if anything his rating is increased round there.

Mags O'Toole (left) receives Tiger Roll's Horse of the Year trophy from Natasha Batterham at Sandown in April 2019

'Wherever possible, why would any handicapper want any horse on a rating he doesn't think is correct?'

Tiger Roll won off 10st 13lb (a BHA mark of 150) in 2018 and 11st 5lb (159) this year and would be attempting to match the three wins of Red Rum, who defied top weight in his last two victories.

Any doubt that Tiger Roll would bid for a third National success in 2020 was removed by Elliott in early September as Matt Butler reported:

Tiger Roll will be targeted at the Randox Health Grand National after Gordon Elliott confirmed the two-time Aintree hero will bid to become the first horse to win the £1 million race for a third consecutive year.

After becoming the first horse to win back-to-back Grand Nationals since Red Rum in April, the line from Tiger Roll's owners Gigginstown House Stud had been the nine-year-old was unlikely to return to Aintree to bid for a historic third consecutive National in a row.

However, in an interview with Aintree racecourse, Tiger Roll's trainer Gordon Elliott confirmed the Grand National on April 4, 2020 is very much on the agenda for his superstar, who will also bid for a fifth Cheltenham Festival success in March.

Elliott thinks Tiger Roll will have an outstanding chance to make history if his preparation goes as planned. He said: 'It's great to see him back, doing a bit of work again. He has had a nice couple of months of summer holidays. He'll probably do three or four weeks of Flat work before he comes back to us in the main yard here.

'Obviously he won't be that busy this year. We're going to have to mind him now and pick and choose where we go. He'll probably have one run over hurdles, maybe something like the Boyne Hurdle [Navan, February] again. He'll go back to Cheltenham [March] for the cross-country race and then we'll go for the Grand National.'

He added: 'I suppose last year we thought he'd hose up until the last 50 yards and he just nearly got caught. I was still confident when he had got past the line last year that he'd won but, until they call the result, you never know.

'This year was probably easier to watch. He travelled and jumped and did everything right. You know, it's a funny thing to say but he was arguably a better horse this year than he was last year.

'I think the build-up to the National this season is going to be unbelievable. The hype - people are talking about him already. Whether he wins, loses or draws, if he gets back there to have a go at three in a row it's going to be great. The hype is going to be brilliant.'

Tiger Roll is one of the highest-rated chasers in training with a mark of 172, but Elliott is not tempted to run him in one of the top Grade 1 races in the jumps calendar.

He said: 'People tell me I should be entering him in Stayers' Hurdles or Gold Cups, but I was always taught and I'm a big believer in going for the race you think you can win at the Cheltenham Festival and the race I think I can win is the cross-country race, so that's where he'll go. But the number one target this season will be the Aintree National.'

Elliott admits he only realised how much his superstar meant to people after his second win in the race. He explained: 'You don't really realise how much the horse meant to everyone. You see all the kids and all the different people who came to the yard.

'You don't really appreciate it when you're in the bubble yourself. You don't realise how much of a thing there is about this horse. It's only after when you sit back and you watch the videos and read all the paper clippings, people have really got to like him.

'You know, he's got a great name and he's got a great heart. Everyone who comes into the yard, there's only one horse they want to see and that's Tiger Roll. He's a people's horse now and we're very lucky to have him.

'Red Rum was before my time but you've seen the videos and heard all about him. He was an amazing horse and to be in the same league as him is unbelievable.'

The connections of Tiger Roll had plenty to feel proud about with two Grand Nationals and four Cheltenham Festival successes in a spectacular career so far. It was therefore welcome news that Tiger Roll would bid for a historic hat-trick in the Aintree showpiece, and victory in April 2020 would be the stuff of legend.

TIGER ROLL: AN APPRECIATION

by ALAN SWEETMAN

Not quite a month old on the day a just-retired warrior led the parade for the 1978 Grand National, Gordon Elliott was born too late to have first-hand memories of Aintree's greatest hero. Red Rum was a celebrity in an age when the word really meant something, a horse known to millions for whom the world of racing was otherwise a matter of indifference.

In April 2019 Tiger Roll took the same great leap from the track into public consciousness in a way no horse has done, other than perhaps Desert Orchid, in the intervening years.

Elliott was too young to recall.

Owner Michael O'Leary has understandably been reluctant to be drawn into comparisons with the ultimate Aintree legend. However, the enormity of the achievement has not been lost on either man, and Davy Russell found a reference point from his formative years to place it in a fitting context.

No-one needed reminding of how the challenge posed by the Aintree fences has changed beyond recognition. Yet in strictly competitive terms the race is far deeper in talent than in the past. More than ever, you need plenty of pace to hold a position.

You still require significant resources of stamina to see out the trip, and rare qualities of agility and athleticism to negotiate the obstacles effectively. The relatively low trajectory of Tiger Roll's jumping style, part of his make-up since early novice wins at Ballinrobe and Kilbeggan, is perfectly suited to the modern Aintree format, just as Red Rum's technique was tailor-made for the old fences.

There was a strong similarity between these two in terms of physical stature and an indefinable sense of character, a sort of swagger and confident self-awareness.

Tommy Stack has often recalled the night after the historic third National win in 1977, when Red Rum was led through the lobby of a Southport hotel and down into the ballroom where he received the vociferous acclaim of his fans with aplomb. Tiger Roll has a similar aura about him.

Both horses had an inauspicious background in Flat racing, but Red Rum holds an edge in that respect. At least he was able to make a modest mark on the Flat at two and three, whereas Tiger Roll failed to make it to the track in the discipline for which he was bred.

Luckily the right people found him along the way. From Nigel Hawke to Mags O'Toole, to Eddie and Michael O'Leary, and to master trainer Elliott and his superb backroom team, with a special mention for Keith Donoghue.

Tiger Roll's versatility has broken the normal rules. From the perspective of his overall race-record, Elliott has achieved one of the great sustained training performances in Irish jump racing history.

A truly exceptional training feat typically involves sequential or collective performances. In an Irish context you could cite three-in-a-row Cheltenham Festival winners including Vincent O'Brien with Cottage Rake and Hatton's Grace, Tom Dreaper with Arkle and Aidan O'Brien with Istabraq. For all the reservations about the quality of the opposition, Willie Mullins deserves due credit for winning the Mares' Hurdle six times with Quevega.

Vincent O'Brien's three successive National victories with Early Mist (1953), Royal Tan (1954) and Quare Times (1955) were phenomenal. As were Dreaper's seven consecutive Irish Grand National winners between 1960 and 1966.

What Elliott has done with Tiger Roll across the range of distances and disciplines is exceptional. A Triumph Hurdle winner is not designed to become a National Hunt Chase winner. A career in cross-country races, other than for horses trained by Enda Bolger or Peter Maher, is usually a halfway house to the retirement pastures.

Tiger Roll made a wondrous transition from Cheltenham to Aintree in 2018. His 'double-double', after thoroughly demolishing a field of perfectly respectable hurdlers in the Boyne Hurdle as part of the warm-up, a year later was astonishing.

Can he add another chapter to the story in 2020? No reason why not. All being well, 11st 10lb should not be a deterrent.

CAREER SUMMARY

RESULTS (AT CLOSE OF 2018–19 SEASON)

TIGER ROLL (IRE)

14 March 2010, bay gelding
Authorized (Ire) – Swiss Roll (Ire) (Entrepreneur) (GB)
TRAINERS: Nigel Hawke and Gordon Elliott
OWNERS: Sheikh Mohammed, Mrs K Wetherall and Gigginstown House Stud
BREEDER: Jerry O'Brien

Jumps placings 121/71P6430/40/P114U2221331P/2P511/4111-
Flat placing 2/

LIFETIME RECORD

	RUNS	WINS	2NDS	3RDS	WINNINGS	EARNINGS	OR	BEST TS	BEST RPR
Chase	20	8	4	2	£1,207,362	£1,227,895	172	173	174
Hurdle	14	4	1	1	£114,926	£137,850	156	139	160
All-weather	1	0	1	0	–	£1,537	–	–	59
Rules races	35	12	6	3	£1,322,287	£1,367,282	–	–	–

DATE	RACE CONDITIONS	WGT	RACE OUTCOME	JOCKEY	OR	TS	RPR
6 Apr 19	Ain 4m2½fGS C1HcChG3 500k	11-5	1/40 (2¾l Magic Of Light 10-11) 4-1f	D Russell	159	173	174
13 Mar 19	Chl 3m6fSft C2Ch 40k	11-4	1/15 (22l Josies Orders 11-4) 5-4f	K Donoghue	159	128	171
17 Feb 19	Nav 2m5fY HG2 24k	11-3	1/6 (4l Off You Go 11-3) 25-1	K Donoghue	140	33	160
16 Nov 18	Chl 3m6fGd C2HcCh 15k	11-12	4/7 (5½l Josies Orders 10-11) 11-4	K Donoghue	159	121	158
14 Apr 18	Ain 4m2½fHy C1HcChG3 500k	10-13	1/38 (hd Pleasant Company 10-11) 10-1	D Russell	150	158	163
14 Mar 18	Chl 3m6fSft C2Ch 40k	11-4	1/16 (2l Urgent De Gregaine 11-4) 7-1	K Donoghue	150	98	153
15 Dec 17	Chl 3m6fGS C2HcCh 22k	11-6	5/9 (42l Bless The Wings 11-2) 7-1	K Donoghue	151	108	118
16 Nov 17	Clo 2m4½fSft/Hy ChG2 26k	11-6	PU/6 (Alpha Des Obeaux 11-4) 20-1	K Donoghue	151	–	–
30 Oct 17	Wex 2m7fSft ChL 15k	11-10	2/5 (1½l A Genie In Abottle 11-4) 11-2	J Kennedy	151	–	151
17 Apr 17	Fai 3m5fGd/Y HcCh 235k	10-13	PU/28 (Our Duke 11-4) 16-1	D Meyler	151	–	–
14 Mar 17	Chl 4mGS C1NvChG2 72k	11-6	1/18 (3l Missed Approach 11-6) 16-1	L O'Neill	152	93	157
31 Oct 16	Wex 2m7fGd ChL 13k	10-13	3/7 (10½l Bay Of Freedom 10-9) 5-2	D Meyler	146	–	131
21 Oct 16	Chl 3m½fGd C2NvCh 13k	11-8	3/6 (4½l Heron Heights 11-8) 6-4f	Mr J Codd	152	72	143
9 Oct 16	Lim 3mY HcCh 44k	10-6	1/15 (8l Stellar Notion 10-3) 20-1	D Meyler	138	134	157
17 Sep 16	Lis 2m4fY NcCh 10k	11-12	2/4 (12l Deans Road 11-7) 6-4	B Cooper	138	–	120
6 Sep 16	Gal 2m2fSft NvChG3 15k	11-5	2/8 (16l Tocororo 9-12) 9-2	B Cooper	138	92	147
18 Aug 16	Kil 2m4½fGd NvCh 7k	11-12	2/6 (1½l Baily Cloud 11-8) 2-1jf	J Kennedy	138	110	138
28 Jul 16	Gal 2m2fGd/Y NvCh 11k	11-9	UR/8 (Xsquared 11-9) 11-4f	B Cooper	138	–	0
12 Jul 16	Kil 2m6½fGd NvCh 9k	11-10	4/6 (7l Sandymount Duke 11-5) 5-2	B Cooper	–	114	142
20 Jun 16	Klb 2m4fGd NvCh 6k	11-8	1/7 (3½l Valyssa Monterg 11-1) 7-4f	J Kennedy	–	108	138
31 May 16	Bal 2m1fGd Ch 5k	11-9	1/12 (8l Buster Dan Dan 11-9) 5-2jf	J Kennedy	–	74	133
30 Apr 16	Pun 2m4fY HcH 44k	11-2	PU/25 (Anibale Fly 10-9) 25-1	B Cooper	142	–	0
9 Apr 16	Ain 3m½fSft C1HcHG3 28k	10-13	14/19 (37l Ubak 11-0) 20-1	B Cooper	145	55	113
23 Mar 16	Dun 2mSt Md 5k	9-10	2/11 (½l Sir Raston 9-5) 9-4	R Cleary	–	–	59
1 May 15	Pun 2mGd/Y HG1 95k	11-12	4/4 (36l Faugheen 11-12) 33-1	B Cooper	146	114	139
12 Mar 15	Chl 3mGd C1HG1 171k	11-10	13/16 (39l Cole Harden 11-10) 50-1	D Condon	150	113	136
14 Feb 15	Gow 2mSft HG2 22k	11-11	3/5 (18l Kitten Rock 11-9) 7-1	B Cooper	149	102	142
25 Jan 15	Lep 2mY HG1 52k	11-8	4/6 (18½l Hurricane Fly 11-10) 33-1	B Cooper	149	77	149
29 Dec 14	Lep 2mSft HG1 51k	11-7	6/7 (19l Hurricane Fly 11-10) 16-1	B Cooper	150	123	135
31 Oct 14	Dwn 2mY HG2 28k	11-6	PU/7 (Little King Robin 10-12) 9-4	B Cooper	150	–	0
18 Oct 14	Chl 2m½fGS C24yH 19k	11-6	1/4 (½l Calipto 10-12) 15-8	B Cooper	150	139	150
3 May 14	Pun 2mGd/Y 4yHG1 53k	11-0	7/13 (12l Abbyssial 11-0) 13-8f	D Russell	147	107	136
14 Mar 14	Chl 2m1fGd C14yHG1 68k	11-0	1/15 (3¼l Kentucky Hyden 11-0) 10-1	D Russell	–	128	144
9 Feb 14	Lep 2mSft/Hy 4yHG1 41k	11-0	2/6 (2¼l Guitar Pete 11-0) 16-1	B Cooper	–	115	136
10 Nov 13	Mar 2m½fSft C43yH 4k	10-9	1/5 (3¾l Nonotnow 10-12) 12-1	M Quinlan	–	62	95